T0328396

EMPOWERED EDUCATORS
IN CHINA

EMPOWERED EDUCATORS IN CHINA

How High-Performing Systems Shape Teaching Quality

Mistilina Sato
with Jiacheng Li

A Wiley Brand

Published by Jossey-Bass
A Wiley Brand

One Montgomery Street, Suite 1000, San Francisco, CA 94104-4594—www.josseybass.com

Jossey-Bass books and products are available through most bookstores. To contact
Jossey-Bass directly call our Customer Care Department within the U.S. at 800-956-7739,
outside the U.S. at 317-572-3986, or fax 317-572-4002.

Wiley publishes in a variety of print and electronic formats and by print-on-demand.
Some material included with standard print versions of this book may not be included
in e-books or in print-on-demand. If this book refers to media such as a CD or DVD
that is not included in the version you purchased, you may download this material at
http://booksupport.wiley.com. For more information about Wiley products, visit
www.wiley.com.

ISBN: 9781119369653
ISBN: 9781119369660
ISBN: 9781119369639

Cover design by Wiley
Cover image: © suriya9/Getty Images, Inc.

Printed in the United States of America
FIRST EDITION
PB Printing   10 9 8 7 6 5 4 3 2 1

CONTENTS

FOREWORD

FEW WOULD DISAGREE THAT, among all the factors that affect how much students learn, the quality of their teachers ranks very high. But what, exactly, do policy makers, universities, and school leaders need to do to make sure that the vast majority of teachers in their jurisdiction are *literally* world class?

Perhaps the best way to answer that question is to look carefully and in great detail at what the countries whose students are performing at the world's top levels are doing to attract the highest quality high school students to teaching careers, prepare them well for that career, organize schools so teachers can do the best work of which they are capable, and provide incentives for them to get better at the work before they finally retire.

It was not hard for us to find the right person to lead a study that would do just that. Stanford professor Linda Darling-Hammond is one of the world's most admired researchers. Teachers and teaching have been lifelong professional preoccupations for her. And, not least, Professor Darling-Hammond is no stranger to international comparative studies. Fortunately for us and for you, she agreed to lead an international comparative study of teacher quality in a selection of top-performing countries. The study, *Empowered Educators: How High-Performing Systems Shape Teaching Quality Around the World*, took two years to complete and is unprecedented in scope and scale.

The volume you are reading is one of six books, including case studies conducted in Australia, Canada, China, Finland, and Singapore. In addition to the case studies and the cross-study analysis, the researchers have collected a range of videos and artifacts (http://ncee.org/empowered-educators)—ranging from a detailed look at how the daily schedules of teachers in Singapore ensure ample time for collaboration and planning to a description of the way Shanghai teachers publish their classroom research in refereed journals—that we hope will be of great value to policy makers and educators interested in using and adapting the tools that the top-performing jurisdictions use to get the highest levels of teacher quality in the world.

Studies of this sort are often done by leading scholars who assemble hordes of graduate students to do the actual work, producing reams of reports framed by the research plan, which are then analyzed by the principal investigator. That is not what happened in this case. For this report, Professor Darling-Hammond recruited two lead researcher-writers for each case study, both senior, one from the country being studied and one from another country, including top-level designers and implementers of the systems being studied and leading researchers. This combination of insiders and external observers, scholars and practitioner-policy makers, gives this study a depth, range, and authenticity that is highly unusual.

But this was not just an effort to produce first-class case studies. The aim was to understand what the leaders were doing to restructure the profession of teaching for top performance. The idea was to cast light on that by examining what was the same and what was different from country to country to see if there were common threads that could explain uncommon results. As the data-gathering proceeded, Professor Darling-Hammond brought her team together to exchange data, compare insights, and argue about what the data meant. Those conversations, taking place among a remarkable group of senior policy actors, practitioners, and university-based researchers from all over the world, give this work a richness rarely achieved in this sort of study.

The researchers examined all sorts of existing research literature on the systems they were studying, interviewed dozens of people at every level of the target systems, looked at everything from policy at the national level to practice in individual schools, and investigated not only the specific policies and practices directly related to teacher quality, but the larger economic, political, institutional, and cultural contexts in which policies on teacher quality are shaped.

Through it all, what emerges is a picture of a sea change taking place in the paradigm of mass education in the advanced industrial nations. When university graduates of any kind were scarce and most people had jobs requiring only modest academic skills, countries needed teachers who knew little more than the average high school graduate, perhaps less than that at the primary school level. It was not too hard to find capable people, typically women, to do that work, because the job opportunities for women with that level of education were limited.

But none of that is true anymore. Wage levels in the advanced industrial countries are typically higher than elsewhere in the world. Employers who can locate their manufacturing plants and offices anywhere in the world and who do not need highly skilled labor look for workers who have the basic skills they need in low-wage countries, so the work available to workers with only the basic skills in the high-wage countries is drying up. That process is being greatly accelerated by the rapid advance of automation. The jobs that are left in the high-wage countries mostly demand a higher level of more complex skills.

These developments have put enormous pressure on the governments of high-wage countries to find teachers who have more knowledge and a deeper command of complex skills. These are the people who can get into selective universities and go into occupations that have traditionally had higher status and are better compensated than school teaching. What distinguishes the countries with the best-performing education systems is that: 1) they have figured this out and focused hard on how to respond to these new realities; and 2) they have succeeded not just in coming up with promising designs for the systems they need but in implementing those systems well. The result is not only profound changes in the way they source, educate, train, and support a truly professional teaching force, but schools in which the work of teachers is very differently organized, the demands on school leaders is radically changed, teachers become not the recipient of a new set of instructions from the "center," but the people who are actually responsible for designing and carrying out the reforms that are lifting the performance of their students every day. Not least important, these systems offer real careers in teaching that enable teachers, like professionals in other fields, to gain more authority, responsibility, compensation, and status as they get better and better at the work, without leaving teaching.

This is an exciting story. It is the story that you are holding in your hand. The story is different in every country, province, and state. But the themes behind the stories are stunningly similar. If you find this work only half as compelling as I have, you will be glued to these pages.

MARC TUCKER, PRESIDENT
NATIONAL CENTER ON EDUCATION AND THE ECONOMY

ACKNOWLEDGMENTS

WORKING IN INTERNATIONAL CONTEXTS as a nonnative requires a lot of support from people who are willing to spend time talking about the basic elements of the system in which they live. Your supporters must have much patience with your naive understanding, and they must be willing to look at their own system with the lens of an outsider trying to understand. I was extremely lucky to find such support through the Institute for Schooling Reform and Development at East China Normal University (ECNU) in Shanghai.

I now count among my colleagues Jiacheng LI, professor of Education Science at ECNU. I am deeply appreciative of his partnership in the research and writing of this case. Dr. LI is a very busy man, yet he took time to meet with me, to set up school visits, to find translators, to read and add text to drafts of the case study that provided valuable insights from an insiders' perspective. I take full responsibility for the information in this case, but want to acknowledge Dr. LI for his contributions that gave nuance and factual accuracy to many facets of the case.

I also want to acknowledge Professor Lan YE, the founding director of the Institute for Schooling Reform and Development at ECNU. Professor YE's groundbreaking work on university-school partnerships has created a catalyst for change in schools, and her writings continue to influence how schools imagine teaching and learning interactions. The two hours I spent with her during an interview helped me grasp the history of teaching in China and the cultural importance of education to the nation. These deeply held values are part of what creates a systemic tension as Shanghai and the Institute for Schooling Reform and Development strive to create a "new" basic education model within the traditional space of a merit-based system with reward for hard work.

Also, Professor Gang DING, dean of the Institute of Advanced Studies in Education at ECNU provided data from his own national study on teacher professional learning to support this case.

I am also very grateful to Ms. Xu (Iris) ZHOU, director of the Office of International Affairs, School of Education Science for being so welcoming to me and my family. Through her office at ENCU, I was able to make all of my arrangements to be a visiting scholar, and Iris provided that personal reassurance that we could make everything work out during my visit.

During my month-long stay in Shanghai in fall 2013, I was privileged to be welcomed into four school sites and the two university teacher preparation programs in Shanghai. Presentations by and interviews with the principals and staff at Shanghai Jiangsu Road No.5 Primary School, Qibao Experimental Junior High School, Pujiang No. 2 Elementary School, and Qilun Elementary School provided essential information for understanding how teachers' work is constructed in China. I sat in on teacher meetings in which lessons were being designed. I attended lessons with several other teachers and parents to watch the instruction and then listen in on the follow-up conversation where the teacher got feedback from peers and parents. I saw lesson plans that were being designed for district level competitions. And I interviewed teachers about their work and professional learning opportunities. In the United States, arranging for visitors to enter classrooms often creates a disruption and requires making special arrangements with a teacher. My hosts in Shanghai certainly went out of their way to arrange meetings and interviews, but my impression of classroom visits and observations was that it was a perfectly normal event to have a group of teachers in the back of the classroom observing the lesson.

Ms. Nianyang WU, deputy director of the Faculty of Education at Shanghai Normal University, hosted a focus group meeting of teacher education candidates and provided an informative overview of the program at Shanghai Normal. Faculty at East China Normal University shared descriptions of the programs at ECNU, and counselors at the new Xiancheng MENG College on the Minhang campus of ECNU met with me to describe the system of support that their teacher candidates have.

Three district administrators made time to talk with me about the Shanghai system of education. Ms. Defang WU, deputy director, Division of Schooling and Lifelong Learning helped me understand the ongoing professional learning opportunities that teachers in Shanghai have. Ms. Yue ZHU, assistant superintendent Minhang District described the hiring process and support for first-year teachers in her district. Mr. Zhiyue GU, senior advisor to the Shanghai Municipal Education Commission and former head of one of the Shanghai Districts, provided insights about how the Shanghai Municipal Education Commission views the PISA results and their current desire for educational reform that makes learning more innovative and creative for students.

Working in a Mandarin-speaking context while being monolingual in English had its own challenges. ECNU provided excellent translation support by recruiting three of their graduate students to travel with me to meetings. Zhongxian CHEN, Yun JI, and Yanting LIU became a constant presence in my ear as they translated meetings proceedings, my interview questions, and located documents. They, themselves, as candidates to become teachers and education officials provided insights into the work and career opportunities in the Chinese education system. When I returned to the University of Minnesota, I had support to translate documents and interview recordings for the final case write-up by Fang (Andie) WANG.

I am very appreciative of the detailed feedback I received from several reviewers on earlier versions of this case. Three reviewers from the Center on International Education Benchmarking International Advisory Board provided helpful insights on how the overall case was or was not capturing elements of the Shanghai and overall China policy system. Thank you to Minxuan ZHANG, professor and director, Research Institute for International and Comparative Education at Shanghai Normal University; Michael Day, professor of Education and director of the School of Education at Roehampton University in the UK, and Kai Ming Cheng, emeritus professor Division of Policy, Administration and Social Sciences Education at Hong Kong University. Professor Cheng was also very helpful during the field study portion of this case development. I had the opportunity to visit him in Hong Kong immediately after my visit to Shanghai to debrief my findings with him and his colleagues. I have made efforts to address all of the reviewers' feedback. Some will be disappointed that there is no simple answer to the question of "why Shanghai performs so well on PISA," but their comments pushed me to better address the multiple contributing factors. In addition, Dion Burns, research analyst and Linda Darling-Hammond, faculty director, both at the Stanford Center for Opportunity Policy in Education, provided detailed comments and suggestions that led to more description of the practices in the schools to give the case more life.

I want to thank Linda Darling-Hammond for presenting me with the opportunity to learn and write about Shanghai. It was a meaningful opportunity to me on many levels. My own passion for understanding, supporting, and developing teaching and teachers made this project a fit that educational researchers dream of. The opportunity to work with such a dynamic team of researchers—many of whom I have admired for decades—made this an experience in which we were all deepening our understanding together. Being part of this team enriched my own thinking and understanding in immeasurable ways.

I took on this work during a sabbatical from the College of Education and Human Development at the University of Minnesota-Twin Cities. My college is very supportive of its faculty, and having the opportunity to explore new lines of research is a gift that will continue to support my career for many years. Being on sabbatical also meant that I could take an extended time to visit Shanghai and have the opportunity to take my family with me. My husband and two children had a life-changing experience with me while we lived in Shanghai and later traveled in greater China. We all became citizens of the world during this family journey.

Learning about China through a Westerners' eyes and ears is a complex task. We take so much for granted about what "school" looks like and how our systems are set up to support schooling practices. Even with a lot of preparatory reading about China and its schools in advance of arriving in Shanghai, I look back on my interviews and school visits and I see how my questions are framed with a western perspective on what I expected to see and learn. Now that I understand more about the Shanghai education system through the support of all of these people, I have a deep impression of their commitment to high-quality education, and their willingness to share their practices is a strong testament to the learning culture I experienced in China.

ABOUT THE SPONSORING ORGANIZATIONS

THIS WORK IS MADE POSSIBLE through a grant by the Center on International Education Benchmarking® of the National Center on Education and the Economy® and is part of a series of reports on teacher quality systems around the world. For a complete listing of the material produced by this research program, please visit www.ncee.org/cieb.

The Center on International Education Benchmarking®, a program of NCEE, funds and conducts research around the world on the most successful education systems to identify the strategies those countries have used to produce their superior performance. Through its books, reports, website, monthly newsletter, and a weekly update of education news around the world, CIEB provides up-to-date information and analysis on those countries whose students regularly top the PISA league tables. Visit www.ncee.org/cieb to learn more.

The National Center on Education and the Economy was created in 1988 to analyze the implications of changes in the international economy for American education, formulate an agenda for American education based on that analysis and seek wherever possible to accomplish that agenda through policy change and development of the resources educators would need to carry it out. For more information visit www .ncee.org.

Research for this volume was coordinated by the Stanford Center for Opportunity Policy in Education (SCOPE) at Stanford University. SCOPE was founded in 2008 to foster research, policy, and practice to advance high-quality, equitable education systems in the United States and internationally.

ABOUT THE AUTHORS

 **Mistilina Sato,** PhD is an associate professor of teacher development and science education at the University of Minnesota-Twin Cities. She is the inaugural holder of the Carmen Starkson Campbell Chair for Innovation in Teacher Development. Her research focuses on teaching across the career continuum, including teacher preparation, performance assessment of teachers, early career induction, teacher evaluation, teacher leadership, and National Board Certification. Sato is currently the co-PI and director of the Teacher Education Redesign Initiative and leads the Teacher Education Research Collaborative in her college. She served on the national design and standards setting team for the edTPA, a nationally available performance assessment for teacher candidates. She has received awards for her research from the National Staff Development Council and AERA Division K—Teaching and Teacher Education. Her work has been published in *American Educational Research Journal,* the *Journal of Teacher Education, Phi Delta Kappan*, and *Educational Leadership.* Sato began her career as a middle school science teacher in New Jersey. She holds a PhD from Stanford University in curriculum and teacher education and a BA from Princeton University in geological sciences.

 **Jiacheng Li,** PhD is a professor of Education Science at the East China Normal University, China. His research focuses on schooling reform, student development, school-family collaboration, and teacher leadership. He has received awards for his research from the Chinese Ministry of Education and Shanghai Municipal Education Commission. Li began his career as an elementary school teacher. He holds a PhD from East China Normal University and an MA from Northeast Normal University, China.

ONLINE DOCUMENTS AND VIDEOS

Access online documents an videos at
http://ncee.org/empowered-educators

Link Number	Description	URL
1-1	Shanghai Parent Committee Observation and Feedback Form	http://ncee.org/2017/01/shanghai-parent-committee-observation-and-feedback-form/
2-1	Shanghai Compulsory Education Law 1986	http://ncee.org/2017/01/shanghai-compulsory-education-law-1986/
2-2	Shanghai Education Law 1995	http://ncee.org/2017/01/shanghai-education-law-1995/
2-3	Shanghai Basic Education Reform and Development 2006	http://ncee.org/2017/01/shanghai-basic-education-reform-and-development-2006/
2-4	China Education Plan 2010-2020	http://ncee.org/2016/12/china-education-plan-2010--2020/
4-1	Duties of Shanghai Municipal Education Commission	http://ncee.org/2017/01/duties-of-shanghai-municipal-education-commission/
5-1	Shanghai Teachers Law 1994	http://ncee.org/2017/01/shanghai-teachers-law-1994/
5-2	Shanghai Teaching Achievement Award Regulations	http://ncee.org/2017/01/shanghai-teaching-achievement-award-regulations/
5-3	Shanghai Teachers' Continuing Ed Requirements	http://ncee.org/2017/01/shanghai-teachers-continuing-ed-requirements/
5-4	Training of Banzhuren	http://ncee.org/2016/12/training-of-banzhuren/

Link Number	Description	URL
5-5	Shanghai Qilun Primary Parent Events	http://ncee.org/2017/01/shanghai-qilun-primary-parent-events/
5-6	Shanghai Qilun Primary School Brochure	http://ncee.org/2017/01/shanghai-qilun-primary-school-brochure/
7-1	Shanghai Teacher Application for Honorary Title	http://ncee.org/2017/01/shanghai-teacher-application-for-honorary-title/
7-2	Qilun Primary Teacher Annual Evaluation	http://ncee.org/2016/12/qilun-primary-teacher-annual-evaluation/
7-3	Qilun Primary Students' Evaluation of Teachers Survey	http://ncee.org/2016/12/qilun-primary-students-evaluation-of-teachers-survey/

THE SURPRISING SUCCESS OF SHANGHAI STUDENTS

IN 2009 SHANGHAI PARTICIPATED for the first time in the Organization for Economic Co-operation and Development's (OECD) triennial Programme for International Student Assessment (PISA). PISA exams are administered to a random sample of 15-year-olds in participating jurisdictions in three subject matter areas: reading, mathematics, and science. Typically, nations, not municipalities, are represented in PISA. In 2009, however, Shanghai was among the 74 jurisdictions and in 2012 it was among the 65 jurisdictions participating in the assessment (Beijing and other Chinese provinces also participated in 2009 but only in an exploratory manner). Shanghai surprised the global education community by scoring at the top of the charts in reading, mathematics, and science in 2009 and then repeating that ranking in the 2012 results. Figure 1.1 shows that Shanghai's students' performance in all three tested areas is well above the OECD average student performance. In addition, Shanghai had the smallest percentage of students performing in the lowest levels of mathematics and the highest percentage of students performing at the highest levels of PISA exams. These results have left many people in the policy and school reform communities asking how Shanghai has managed to create a system that supports its students to perform so well on these measures of student achievement.

One typical response[1] to explaining Shanghai students' performance on PISA exams is that the Asian educational approach is based primarily on memorization, repetition, and exam preparation. Certainly, exam preparation helps a great deal and there is no doubt that students in Shanghai learn how to prepare for exams. However, the PISA tests are not directly linked to school curriculum. The tests are "designed to assess to what extent students at the end of compulsory education, can apply their knowledge to real-life situations and be equipped for full participation in society . . . The tests are a mixture of open-ended and multiple-choice

Figure 1.1 Snapshot of performance in mathematics, reading, and science

	Mathematics				Reading		Science	
	Mean score in PISA 2012	Share of low-achievers (Below Level 2)	Share of top-performers in mathematics (Level 5 or 6)	Annualised change	Mean score in PISA 2012	Annualised change	Mean score in PISA 2012	Annualised change
OECD average	494	23.1	12.6	-0.3	496	0.3	501	0.5
Shanghai-Chine	613	3.8	55.4	4.2	570	4.6	580	1.8
Singapore	573	8.3	40.0	3.8	542	5.4	551	3.3
Hong Kong-China	561	8.5	33.7	1.3	545	2.3	555	2.1
Chinese Taipei	560	12.8	37.2	1.7	523	4.5	523	-1.5
Korea	554	9.1	30.9	1.1	536	0.9	538	2.6
Macao-China	538	10.8	24.3	1.0	509	0.8	521	1.6
Japan	536	11.1	23.7	0.4	538	1.5	547	2.6
Liechtenstein	535	14.1	24.8	0.3	516	1.3	525	0.4
Switzerland	531	12.4	21.4	0.6	509	1.0	515	0.6
Netherlands	523	14.8	19.3	-1.6	511	-0.1	522	-0.5
Estonia	521	10.5	14.6	0.9	516	2.4	541	1.5
Finland	519	12.3	15.3	-2.8	524	-1.7	545	-3.0
Canada	518	13.8	16.4	-1.4	523	-0.9	525	-1.5
Poland	518	14.4	16.7	2.6	518	2.8	526	4.6
Belgium	515	18.9	19.4	-1.6	509	0.1	505	-0.8
Germany	514	17.7	17.5	1.4	508	1.8	524	1.4
Viet Nam	511	14.2	13.3	m	508	m	528	m
Austria	506	18.7	14.3	0.0	490	-0.2	506	-0.8
Australia	504	19.7	14.8	-2.2	512	-1.4	521	-0.9
Ireland	501	16.9	10.7	-0.6	523	-0.9	522	2.3
Slovenia	501	20.1	13.7	-0.6	481	-2.2	514	-0.8
Denmark	500	16.8	10.0	-1.8	496	0.1	498	0.4
New Zealand	500	22.6	15.0	-2.5	512	-1.1	516	-2.5
Czech Republic	499	21.0	12.9	-2.5	493	-0.5	508	-1.0
France	495	22.4	12.9	-1.5	505	0.0	499	0.6
United Kingdom	494	21.8	11.8	-0.3	499	0.7	514	-0.1
Iceland	493	21.5	11.2	-2.2	483	-1.3	478	-2.0
Latvia	491	19.9	8.0	0.5	489	1.9	502	2.0
Luxembourg	490	24.3	11.2	-0.3	488	0.7	491	0.9
Norway	489	22.3	9.4	-0.3	504	0.1	495	1.3
Portugal	487	24.9	10.6	2.8	488	1.6	489	2.5
Italy	485	24.7	9.9	2.7	490	0.5	494	3.0
Spain	484	23.6	8.0	0.1	488	-0.3	496	1.3
Russian Federation	482	24.0	7.8	1.1	475	1.1	486	1.0
Slovak Republic	482	27.5	11.0	-1.4	463	-0.1	471	-2.7
United States	481	25.8	8.8	0.3	498	-0.3	497	1.4

OECD, 2014, p. 5.

questions that are organised in groups based on a passage setting out a real-life situation" (OECD, n.d.). Based on the rigor and design of the test questions, rote memorization of school texts is not Shanghai's secret to success. When interviewed about Shanghai's performance on the 2009 PISA exams, Andreas Schleicher, the PISA program's designer at OECD, summarized:

> Shanghai's education system is distinctive and superior—and not just globally, but also nationally. Hong Kong, Beijing, and ten Chinese provinces participated in the 2009 PISA, but their results reflected education systems that were still the same-old knowledge acquisition models, whereas Shanghai had progressed to equipping students with the ability to interpret and extrapolate information from text and apply it to real world situations—what we would normally refer to as "creativity." Twenty-six percent of Shanghai 15-year-olds could demonstrate advanced problem-solving skills, whereas the OECD average is 3 percent.

> (Jiang, 2011)

Many other factors seem to be at play within the overall Shanghai system, including the students' motivation toward strong performance, the parental support for education that is culturally engrained throughout the country, the focus that the teachers place on high expectations for students and the individual tutoring they provide (sometimes without additional pay and sometimes with a consulting fee) (Tan, 2013). These cultural values for education in general and the role of adults in supporting the younger generations toward their educational potential and success in life are well accepted as partially explaining the high performance of several Asian countries on international comparison exams (Cheng, 2014).

Beyond the cultural explanation that education is the "key to social mobility" for the individual who works hard, Cheng (2014) points out that the cultural value for education is represented also in the financial and policy investments in expanding and improving the educational systems serving vast populations of children. With this systems frame in mind, the question that follows from the Shanghai results is: How is the educational system—its culture, policies, and practices—set up to support the kind of student performance we see in the Shanghai results? In particular, how does the system structure teaching, and the role and quality of teachers, to contribute to these outcomes?

This Study

In the text that follows, I attempt to do two things in order to answer these questions. I describe the national geographic and economic context of China, the nation's policy reforms over time that built the modern Chinese educational system, and the educational practices that are considered typical in China. I give primary focus to policies and practices that contribute to the preparation, hiring, and ongoing professional support for teachers within the system based on the assumption that teachers are a key feature of the education system that contributes to student performance and achievement (this assumption is also explicitly stated within Chinese law).

I then delve into specific descriptions of how these national policies are translated, adapted, and enacted in Shanghai. The case of Shanghai allows us to see an illustration of an educational system that has been investing in educating a diverse student population for three decades and, by measures of international comparison tests, is achieving success. Certainly, Shanghai does not represent the educational practices and conditions in all corners of China. The limited local resources of the western villages create a very different educational context than the densely populated urban throng of Shanghai. Since the early part of the 19th century Shanghai has been a center for international business, shifting over time from industry to finance. Yet, Shanghai is but one of several urban metropolises in China that is working toward educational improvement through experimentation with new curriculum and teaching practices. And Shanghai operates its educational system under the same national laws and within the same cultural traditions as the rest of China. As a large economic center that has a history of innovation and international exposure, I will treat Shanghai as a case of seeing the possibilities of what a developing nation can accomplish within its educational systems.

To construct this text, I drew on several sources of information. I summarize national laws and regulations of China retrieved from the national Ministry of Education website. I also draw on published refereed research, data from national surveys and reports, summaries of the educational context and policies in China and Shanghai published by organizations such as OECD, UNESCO, the Asia Society, and NCEE, and news accounts of policy launches and public reaction. Finally, I conducted field research in Shanghai for four weeks in November 2013. I was generously hosted by higher education colleagues at East China Normal University who made arrangements for me to visit schools and interview teachers, principals, education officials, and university professors and students in education. I also observed classrooms, teacher meetings, and a parent feedback session (Link 1-1).

As an education professor in the United States, I was well aware that I was entering new cultural territory as well as a political system that would be hard to interpret through my Western lived experience. I had some concept of schooling experience in China being driven by examinations, that classrooms had more students than I typically experienced in the US, and that teachers spent less time with children in their typical work week than US teachers. These characteristics are oft-repeated in Western conversations about Chinese education. I was not, however, prepared to understand how deeply the school structure of China influences the overall educational experience of children, or to appreciate the collective nature of teaching within schools, or to grasp the enormous challenges of managing a national school system that serves 200 million children. These elements of Chinese education are described in more detail in the text that follows.

NOTES

1. A discussion of claims that Shanghai excluded migrant children from rural provinces who live in the city from its public schools and from the PISA sample follows in later sections.

2

SITUATING SHANGHAI IN CHINA'S NATIONAL EDUCATION POLICY CONTEXT

THE PEOPLE'S REPUBLIC OF CHINA (PRC) is governed by the Communist Party with the collaboration and support from eight additional parties. The PRC includes 5 ethnic autonomous regions, 22 provinces, 4 province-level municipalities (Beijing, Chongqing, Shanghai, and Tianjin), and 2 primarily self-governing special administrative regions (Macao and Hong Kong). Provinces and ethnic autonomous regions are further divided into administrative units of prefectures, counties, towns, and villages. Municipalities are divided into districts (e.g., Shanghai comprises 16 districts and one county) which are then also divided into township-level divisions and subdistricts.

According to the World Bank, China is the world's most populous country, with a population of 1.36 billion people (mainland China only). By comparison, the United States, the world's third most populous country, has 316.1 million people, a quarter of the number of people in China. China's population comprises 56 different ethnic groups that are officially recognized. However, 92% of Chinese identify within the Han Chinese group. The other ethnic groups are growing at a faster rate than Han Chinese but, because the Han are overwhelmingly dominant in the population, these increases are not expected to dramatically alter China's ethnic composition.

The people of China are almost evenly distributed across urban and rural regions, with 47% of the population living in urban areas and 53% in rural areas. However, the vast deserts of the west and the mountains in the south create an urban population concentration in the eastern coastal cities, such as Shanghai. Since the 1990s, mass migration from rural areas to urban centers has been driven by people's search for better economic opportunities in manufacturing jobs and other rapidly developing

Figure 2.1 Migration patterns within mainland
China show the mass migration from the western
rural provinces to the eastern coastal provinces

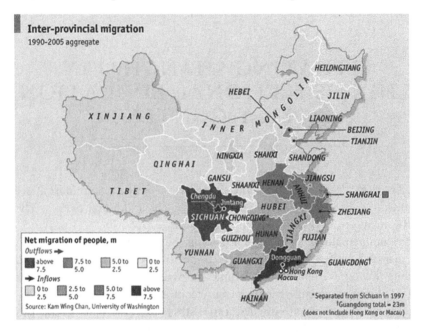

We like to move it move it, 2012.

industries (see Figure 2.1) and Shanghai feels the effects of this migration
on its economy and school infrastructure.

The national migrant population in China reached 245 million people in 2013, representing 18% of the total population (United Nations
Children's Fund, 2014). In Shanghai, the migrant population reached
almost 10 million people (Shanghai Municipal Statistics Bureau, 2015).
The internal national migration is almost a third of all people globally
estimated by the UN to be migrating within the borders of their own
country (We like to move it move it, 2012). This migration is sometimes
referred to as the largest human migration in world history.

This migration has significant impact on the school experience of
China's children. According to the All-China Women's Federation
(2013), 28 percent of children between 6- and 11-years-old and 13%
of children between 12- and 14-years-old in city schools across the
nation are migrants. Two-thirds of those children are with their parents
in cities, and the rest are in their home villages with extended family
while their parents work in the cities (OECD, 2010, p. 96). For those

who are with their parents in cities outside of their home province, the children's ability to attend school can be compromised due to household registration regulations that can limit access to public schools to only those who are legally registered in the city (this will be discussed in greater detail later).

Education Financing in China

China has experienced a history of concentrating resources in the eastern part of the mainland country, creating disproportionate spending on infrastructure and services in the east compared to the west. Since 2000, the Chinese government has been trying to enact new policies to bring better balance to resource distribution between the industrial east and the western countryside and close the gap in regional economic development. Programs such as the Western Development Plan, the Rise of Central China Plan, and the Northeast Revitalization Plan have spurred a narrowing of the gross domestic product (GDP) per capita across provinces and poorer provinces have seen much growth in physical capital (World Bank, 2014). In 2014, the National New Urbanization Plan (2014–2020) was published, which may open more doors to urbanization in China along with more migration to city centers. This will undoubtedly place additional stresses on the social support infrastructure within cities, including the need for education for both adults and children.

China has been investing in the quality and distribution of educational resources through increased overall spending on education for more than 20 years, exceeding the rates of new investment of other developed nations. According to data from OECD, 16.3% of China's total public expenditure was earmarked for educational institutions and public subsidies to households and other private entities for all levels of education in 2011. As a point of reference, Figure 2.2 shows that same year, the US spent 13.8% of total public expenditure on education and the OECD average was 12.9% (OECD, 2011).

In relationship to the GDP of the nation, China has experienced an increasing rate of spending in an effort to keep up with spending in OECD countries as shown in Figure 2.3. In 1993 the central government set a target for education spending at 4% of its GDP by 2000, setting this goal to match the rate of spending on education at the OECD average spending level (Chen, 2012). In 2008, China spent 3.3% of its GDP on education as compared to the OECD average of 5.9%. In 2011, China spent 3.9% of its GDP on education as compared to the OECD average of 6.2% (Roberts, 2013) and in 2012, Premier Wen Jiabao announced that the target for the following year would be 4%, finally allowing China to

Figure 2.2 Percentage of total public expenditures for all levels of education in 2011

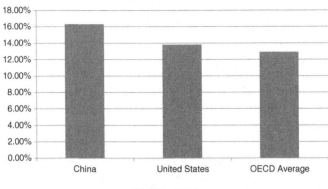

OECD, 2011.

successfully meet its original target goals (Chen, 2012). It is important to note that this increase in GDP percentage spent on education is in the context of China's increasing GDP as a nation, meaning that China's real dollar spending is also sharply on the rise.

Figure 2.3 China's education spending from 2002–2011 as a percentage of its GDP

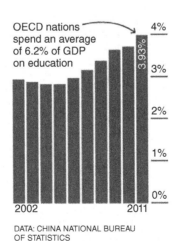

OECD nations spend an average of 6.2% of GDP on education

3.93%

DATA: CHINA NATIONAL BUREAU OF STATISTICS

Roberts, 2013.

In real dollars, China's total spending on education (national, provincial, and local) in 2001 was less than $50 billion USD. Ten years later, that figure has multiplied by five, surpassing $250 billion USD as shown in Figure 2.4 (New York Times, 2013). The 2013 expenditures were projected to be over $300 billion USD (Chen, 2012). Per student spending, on the other hand is the lowest per capita spending on education within the OECD. China spent $1593 USD in 2008, as compared to the OECD average of $8,831USD (NCEE, based on OECD data). This low per capita rate may be explained by the very large student population that China serves in conjunction with the lower personnel salaries within the system as compared to other nations.

Funding for schools was decentralized in the 1986 Compulsory Education Law (Link 2-1), establishing education financing in China across the national, provincial, county, and local township levels. In 2012 only 17.2% of China's total education budget was from the central government, with the rest from local funds. Schools can also receive funding from private enterprises in the form of donations or through school fees for senior secondary without being classified as private schools. The decentralized funding scheme created great inequities across the nation as rural areas were not able to collect and allocate the same resources as urban business centers. In some cases, local townships are unable to pay their teachers and are requiring teachers to pay into their pension plans. This is controversial because, by law, teachers are supposed to be

Figure 2.4 China's investment in education
based on data from UNESCO shows an increase
from less than $50 billion to over $250 billion USD
between 2001 and 2011

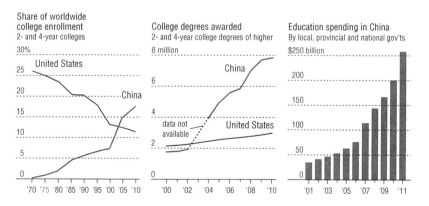

New York Times, 2013 based on UNESCO data.

classified as civil servants and eligible for local government-sponsored pensions. As recently as December 2014, thousands of teachers have been going on strike across a dozen cities in China due to low salaries, underpayment, and the controversial pension payment requirement (China Labor Bulletin, 2014).

The national government has spent the past 15 to 20 years trying to ensure better distribution in spending and resources across the nation. A key strategy has been to better resource the poorer, western provinces with more central government funding. Between 2010 and 2012, the central government increased funding in the west by 550 million Yuan (about $88 million USD). These funds are used to support compulsory education in rural areas through free textbooks, boarding schools in the western and central regions of the country, school nutrition programs, senior secondary enrollment subsidies, college scholarships, improving school conditions, and increasing teacher salaries. Another key effort has been to provide training opportunities for teachers and through setting up model classrooms in rural areas.

In addition to national budget allocations and local resourcing for schooling expenses, many families spend a considerable sum on education. Nationally, families spend about 11% of their total household income on their child's education (China Household Finance Survey, 2013). Families in the urban centers spend more on their children's education—on average 7,808 Yuan ($1301 USD)—compared to the national average of 2,970 Yuan ($495 USD). Given these numbers, Shanghai families are likely investing substantially in their children's education.

Building and Reforming China's Educational System through Policy

The education system within China grows out from the national policy set forth in decisions, law, regulations, and national reform plans established by the State Council and the Communist Party Central Committee. Given the strong single-party system of the Chinese government and the unifying force that the national law provides within the country, it is important to understand how Shanghai's education system is situated within the overall national policy context. The innovative spirit of Shanghai's education system has sometimes influenced the reforms supported at the national level, but the operations of the Shanghai educational system must align with the expectations set out in national law. Therefore, as we explore how the educational system is set up to support the kind of student performance we see in the Shanghai PISA results,

I begin with the national policy reforms that set the expectations for who attends school, the curricular substance of schooling that teachers are responsible for teaching, how teachers are viewed within national policies, how teachers' work is structured, and the performance expectations for teachers.

China has a strong cultural tradition of recognizing the importance of education that dates back centuries. Throughout Chinese history, the Confucius educational traditions of a highly personalized and individual learning process along with examinations that Emperors used to select state officials allowed opportunity for the masses to advance through self-study, individual motivation, and family honor. In 1904, China established its modern school system based on models from Western countries in an effort to bring more systematic opportunities for education to the populace. The development of the national education system since its establishment was interrupted by war and political movements in the early and mid-20th century. Thirty years ago, the Chinese education system began a new period of reform leading to the modern educational system that is funded and run systemically across the nation. Today, China is attempting to educate 200 million children within a system of formal schooling while competing within a global economy.

When China entered the industrial and finance markets of the West after the Cultural Revolution ended in the 1970s, its leaders began to advance an educational system that would be available to all citizens. The early efforts of the national and provincial governments in the 1980s were to establish an educational system with schools and a State-approved curriculum through a nine-year compulsory education requirement. As school attendance became more prevalent across the nation, the national government turned its policy efforts toward improving the quality of the education experiences in schools in the 1990s by enacting laws that set qualifications for teachers, strengthened the expectations for local financing of schools, and established goals for increasing participation in higher education. The development of a national educational system across such a wide expanse of land and across such disparity in economic conditions has proven challenging for China. Reforms in the early 2000s focused on increasing access to quality education to the people in the western countryside and enacting policies to improve the quality of school infrastructure and teacher qualifications in these poorer areas of the country. Current reform efforts continue to address the issue of equity that the nation faces as well as efforts to expand the curricular focus of schools and address the stressful burdens that students experience due the pressures of competition and examinations.

In the following discussion, I summarize some of China's key laws and regulations that have guided China's education reformation over the past 30 years. In this summary, I try to stay close to the original text of the law (in its English translation) in order to illustrate how Chinese values for teaching and education are formalized into State policy. I do this especially for Western readers because in my reading of other summaries of Chinese policy with regard to Shanghai, I found little discussion of how Shanghai's education system sits within the national press toward quality and equity. I also found that sometimes summaries of the national policy in China are oversimplified and aligned with Western language, thus losing some of the value-laden language of the policy within the Chinese cultural context. If we are seeking an answer to how Shanghai's educational system is set up to support strong student performance, I want us to pay particular attention to how teachers are described and treated culturally and in law within China.

Establishing the Modern Chinese School System: 1986 Compulsory Education Law

Under the rule of Mao Zedong, the entire Chinese educational system was dismantled during the Chinese Cultural Revolution (1966–1976) that aimed to purge the bourgeois and capitalist influences from Chinese culture and economy. After Mao's death in 1976, Deng Xiaoping took leadership and began the long process of reestablishing China's economic and educational systems. China first began to rebuild economically by opening its doors to foreign investors and creating manufacturing centers strategically located in its port cities. When China was ready to turn its attention to rebuilding its education system, it faced very high rates of illiteracy and almost two generations of its population who had little or no formal education opportunities. Those who aspired to government leadership were encouraged to seek education outside of the country during this rebuilding era and in 2006, 80% of China's top leadership had been educated in the West (National Center for Economics and Education, n.d.).

In 1985, *The Decision of the Central Committee of the Communist Party of China on the Reform of Education System* heralded the rebirth of China's modern education system. In this decision, government roles were established and the financial policy was determined. In 1986, China passed *The Law on Nine-Year Compulsory Education*.[1] This law required the people's congress within the provincial and autonomous regions to create a nine-year local school system "in accordance with the degree of economic and cultural development in their own localities" and within the guidelines set by the State Council. Children were expected to enroll in school at the age of six "regardless of sex, nationality or race." This "Basic Education" standard for the nation includes six primary years and three junior secondary years of education.

After the nine years of compulsory education, senior secondary schools are available and have shared-cost mechanisms to pay for tuition. To ensure that students from low-income families have access to senior secondary schooling and opportunities to pursue higher education, the government initiated financial support programs through scholarships, work-study programs, subsidies for students with special economic difficulties, tuition reduction or exemption, and state stipends.

In order to ensure that children were available to attend school for their first nine years, the Compulsory Education Law stipulated that "No organization or individual shall employ school-age children or adolescents who should receive compulsory education." The Compulsory Education Law also established Putonghua (the Chinese language based on Beijing pronunciation) as the language of school with the concession that "schools in which the majority of students are of minority nationalities may use the spoken and written languages of those nationalities in instruction."

The overall approach to establishing this new school system was to fund and develop it locally under the overarching authority of the central government. Thus, responsibilities for the development of the school system cascaded through the governing administrative levels. At the provincial level, authorities developed plans, made the rules for the system, and distributed funds to counties while maintaining some key senior secondary schools directly under provincial authority. County-level administration distributed funds to township governments and were also responsible for senior secondary school curriculum, teacher training and in-service development, and agricultural or vocational schools. Townships had to manage the local compulsory primary and junior secondary schools and ensure that any funding needs that were not met by national, provincial, or county funding were gathered locally. This approach to funding the school system still exists today. The law made an allowance that the central government would "subsidize those areas that are unable to introduce compulsory education because of financial difficulties" and "assist areas inhabited by minority nationalities to implement compulsory education by providing them with teachers and funds."

The Compulsory Education Law also set procedures for the preparation of teachers as well as the regard with which teachers would be held locally and nationally. The law expected all primary school teachers to have Normal School education training at the senior secondary level (the equivalent of a senior high school degree). Junior and senior secondary teachers were to have at least higher Normal School education, which is postsecondary training in a school specifically designed to prepare teachers. The law established a system to test for teaching qualifications and described the ideal expectation was for "teachers to make education their long-term career." Additionally, the law expressed that "teachers should be respected by the public. The State shall safeguard the teachers' lawful rights and interests, and take measures to raise their social status and improve their material benefits. It shall reward outstanding educational workers."

As a result of this 1986 law, China saw the slow and deliberate development of schools and teachers, although this development was not uniform across the country. Larger cities and areas in the more developed coastal and southeastern areas of China reached universal nine-year education very quickly as they were already on that path prior to the law being passed. For example, in 1986 Shanghai already had universal attendance at the elementary and junior secondary levels and most students continued on into senior secondary education if all modes of education including vocational schools are counted (Cheng & Yip, 2006). By the early 1990s cities in other economically developed areas of the country, comprising about 25% of China's population, provided nine years of education for all of its children. By 1995, towns and villages with medium-level economic development were on track to provide nine years of compulsory schooling. The full intention of the law, to accelerate and invest in the educational opportunities for children in rural and undeveloped areas in the countryside, took longer to achieve.

Today, China has been successful in enrolling all of its children in schools and compulsory education is now the norm in urban and rural areas. In 2011, the gross enrollment ratio for first grade (the number of new entrants in the first grade regardless of age expressed as a percentage of the eligible population) was 110% for females and 109% for males (World Bank, 2015; note that since this percentage is based on enrollment regardless of age, the percentages can be greater than 100% if children who are younger or older than the eligible age for first grade are enrolled). This number has steadily increased since 2008. Overall, primary school enrollment in 2011 was 113% of the total eligible population (World Bank, 2015). Also according to World Bank statistics from 2010, nine years of compulsory schooling has resulted in a literacy rate of 94% for people ages 15 and above.

Since 2008 compulsory education has been free in China. There is, however, reported practice of charging unauthorized fees for entry into certain schools, for specialized classes, or for preferential treatment of students within schools. Some families pay these fees to schools, to teachers, or to third parties who assist families in securing placements in high performing or selective schools. The Ministry of Education is making an effort to halt these unauthorized fees, but families who want their children to be competitive for places in the most prestigious senior secondary schools and universities continue to pay these additional fees in hopes that the family effort will create greater possibilities of success for their children.

Seeking Educational Improvement: 1995 Education Law

Nine years after compulsory education was in place, the central government turned its attention to improving the quality of schooling and establishing education as the "foundation for construction of socialist modernization." In 1993, the *Chinese Education Reform and Development Outline* emphasized that the education system should meet the demands of economic system reform, and called for schooling reform to move away from "exam-oriented education" and toward "quality education" that would emphasize critical thinking, creativity, and student innovation (CPC Central Committee and the State Council, 1993). This reform plan led to a continuing focus on schooling reforms in policy and in practice.

The *1995 Education Law of the People's Republic of China* (Link 2-2) served as a rallying call for the nation to "pay attention and render support to the educational undertakings," reminds the people that "the whole society shall respect teachers," and demands that "the People's government at different levels, self-managed mass organizations at grassroots level, and organizations in enterprises and institutions shall take every measure to develop education to eliminate illiteracy."

The law approaches educational improvement through establishing processes that control for rigor and accountability within the educational systems. In this policy, the government decreed that the provinces should create a vocational education and adult education system, adopt a national examination system, adopt a schooling credentials system, adopt an academic degree system, and adopt an educational inspection/assessment system for schools and other educational institutions. The law establishes an expectation that educational development be based on scientific research on education and that the nation was now establishing a "scientific school system." The law also established that national awards would be given to organizations and individuals who have made distinguished contributions to education.

The Education Law recognized the important role of teachers and stipulated that national and local governments should "improve the working and living conditions of teachers and raise the social status of teachers." The policy allowed for and encouraged the adoption of "modern means in teaching and learning" and expected that quality of teachers would be strengthened through "examination, rewards, cultivation and training." Evaluation of teachers was to be based on their professional skills.

The 1995 Education Law continued the expectation that the administrative operations of the primary and secondary school system would be at the province and county levels and further specified that higher education would be managed by the provinces and autonomous regions directly under the guidance of the central government. For school system funding, the law stipulated that the national, provincial, county, and municipal governments would establish specific funds to assist "outlying and poverty-stricken areas and areas inhabited by minority ethnic groups in enforcing compulsory education there." Funds were to be raised through local taxes and levies as well as donations, local fundraising efforts and loans. Providing financial support to students from poor families was an expectation for the national government, as well as for society overall based on this new law.

Finally, as China was opening its doors to the west, the central government began encouraging learning abroad more formally through its education system. Foreign exchange programs and international cooperation in education were supported, with the specific values of "independence, equality, mutual benefit and mutual respect." Programs included study abroad for research, academic exchange, and teaching and allowing people from outside of China to teach and engage in research activities inside the country.

Expanding Access to Educational Opportunities: Reform in 2001

By 2001, China declared progress toward the elimination of illiteracy through its Compulsory Education Law. However, the government aimed to improve the basic education quality due to "uneven development and local inadequate attention" and the desire to increase rates of

participation beyond compulsory education through its *2001 Education Plan* (Link 2-3). The State Council adopted a six-point plan for how to further reform and develop the national Basic Education system.

First, the plan carried forward the theme of socialist modernization and made strong claims to the importance of education to China's economic future. The plan set a goal of 90% junior secondary school enrollment rate, 60% senior secondary enrollment rate, and a 95% young adult literacy rate. Overall, the government set a target: "By 2010, the overall level of basic education will approach or reach the level of moderately developed countries."

Second, the plan proposed to provide better systems to "guarantee funding to promote the sustainable and healthy development of rural compulsory education." One of the main areas of financial reform within this law was a call to ensure that teachers in rural areas received their salary and that the counties have appropriate funds and fund management systems to provide these salaries. The reform plan also allowed for tax reform in rural areas and called for the elimination of school fees. To assist rural areas with the issue of school fees that families cannot afford, the western areas of the country were allowed to pilot a system of free textbooks to alleviate this burden from families.

The third point of the plan focused on curriculum reform. While the plan advocated for strengthening the socialist ideology and national patriotism, it also addressed the need to adapt curriculum to children's developmental needs and the overall technological progress of the world. The plan called for curriculum that would "guide students to actively learn," provide for integrated curriculum in core subject areas, allow students to engage in practical activities, and allow for senior secondary elective courses. Primary and secondary schools were encouraged to provide strong science and technology activities to help students develop an interest in science. Curriculum in rural areas was to be based on the "development of modern agriculture and rural industrial structure" and provide an integrated science and agriculture curriculum along with basic education. The "Green Certificate" was established as a pilot program in order to promote the combination of agricultural and technology. Physical health is a common curriculum area in Chinese schools and the basic education reform required one hour each day of sports activity. Arts education was also identified in the reform plan, with a call to improve teaching quality, tap local arts education resources, and for local governments to ensure the necessary conditions for arts education in schools.

Accompanying the Education Plan in 2001 was the development of the Program of Action for Curriculum Reform of Basic Education. This program established new curriculum standards for the subject in basic education, identifying the knowledge, skills, processes, methods, attitudes, and values that students were to learn in each core subject. These new standards, with a focus on improving the quality of education, brought stronger focus to "innovation spirit and practice abilities of students, attach more attention to cultivation of their initiatives, encourage their creative thinking, and explore the interest and potential of youth and teenagers, and foster their curiosity and aspiration to knowledge." By 2006, 10 provinces had adopted the new curricula for senior secondary schools (UNESCO, 2011).

As had been required in law already, the 2001 Education Plan reiterated that textbooks must be approved by the State Council and provincial administrative departments in order to ensure alignment with the national curriculum. Locally developed materials must be validated by the provincial education authorities. New in this reform plan was the specific attention identifying teaching approaches to be promoted:

> Continue to focus on the basics, teaching basic skills and attention to emotions, attitudes culture; take advantage of a variety of curriculum resources, cultivate students' ability to collect, process and use information; conduct research study, students ask questions, study and solve problems; to encourage cooperative learning and promote mutual exchanges between students and common development, promote the teaching and learning of teachers and students. To establish educational reform throughout the region and experiment, explore, and promote new curriculum materials and advanced teaching methods.

Students' academic well-being was addressed in the reform plan in several ways. The academic burden on students was addressed with a call to lighten their load, especially with regard to time spent out of school on school work. Instead, extracurricular activities were to be provided to enrich students' school lives. Development of students' potential and ways to help students build self-confidence were identified. The traditional practice of posting student's rank order in the class based on test results in the classroom was prohibited, although this practice continues today in classrooms. A call for reforming testing practices by developing more complex examination systems that allow students to show what they can do in practical problems and not just what they know was accompanied by the recommendation to reform the college entrance examination and selection system by giving special consideration to students with talents in scientific research, invention, and other outstanding achievements.

Finally, the curriculum reforms called for increased attention to technological changes by better equipping schools with multimedia teaching equipment, educational software, and better access to the Internet. The reform plan recommended seeking support through partnerships with business and industry for schools to upgrade their information technology, laboratories, libraries, sports, and art facilities.

The fourth point of the six-point Education Plan focused on the preparation and support of teachers and is identified as the "key to push forward the quality education." The plan makes general recommendations for the improvements of teachers' colleges and encouraging comprehensive university and other non-normal colleges and universities to engage in the preparation of teachers. All of higher education was called on to support the development of teachers for the western part of the country. The plan set the expectation that improving the overall quality of the teaching workforce should be connected to increasing the training expectations of teachers with some emphasis on supporting more senior secondary teacher development. To address the shortage of teachers in the west, the plan proposed that the poorer areas of the country provide free training for teachers. Specifically, the plan called for increasing the training in information technology, foreign languages, art, and integrated courses. For practicing teachers, the plan made strong statements about the need for improved teacher performance evaluation and mechanisms for dismissing teachers who are not performing their duties well. The need to strengthen principal training and evaluation is also identified in the plan.

The fifth point of the reform plan focused on how to promote the focus on education and the reform plan throughout the nation through community resources. Promoting kindergarten, teacher evaluation, private school development, and the continued development of senior secondary school was a high priority of the government in this reform plan. The plan encouraged the active use of recognition awards to promote education initiatives and encouraged schools to establish awards to advance this reform agenda. The government encouraged local governments to seek local donations through nonprofit groups and state organizations as well as taxes to promote these education initiatives.

The sixth and final point of the plan was to strengthen leadership in these reform efforts. The plan encouraged leaders at all levels to visit schools in order to understand the local situation and be better guides in helping the schools address their issues. The plan called for improving the educational supervision system that would ensure the quality of schooling across the nation with special attention to the economically poor areas. Within this point, the plan proposes family education initiatives established with civic and community organizations with the goal of "healthy growth of young students in the community environment."

Addressing National Equity Issues: Compulsory Education Law Revisited in 2006

In 2006, the central government readopted the national *Compulsory Education Law*. The new law reemphasized that "school-age children and adolescents, regardless of gender, ethnicity, race, family, property status, religious belief, shall enjoy the right to equal access to compulsory education." While children already had access to schools and certified teachers based on previous laws, in many areas of the country schools charged fees for attendance and expected families to provide school materials. Funding for schools in villages and rural areas was not in parity with those in economically developed areas. In the larger cities, where schools are more available and competition is very high due to larger populations, families pay placements fees to ensure that their children have access to the best schools or the best teachers. One of the key efforts of this 2006 law was to address these inequities. For example, the law cracks down on the practices of charging fees and clearly states in its general provisions that in the implementation of compulsory education, schools should not charge tuition fees.

To further this agenda of equalizing educational opportunities for children, the law specifies that local governments above the county level should be responsible for the allocation of educational resources and therein lay the responsibility for providing balanced development of compulsory education across all sectors. The law expected these government authorities to improve school conditions for weak schools, take measures to support educational development in the rural areas, ensure the implementation of compulsory education in ethnic minority areas, and provide financial support to families with financial difficulties. The law encouraged national organizations and economically developed areas to support the implementation of compulsory education in under-developed areas. To "narrow the gap" in the quality of schools, the law abolished the idea of labeling schools as "key schools"—a practice that had been used to establish model organizations that set the example for others to follow. These schools had received additional resources and became highly competitive for student enrollment.

Another equity concern that the law addressed was the prevention of adolescents from dropping out of school. On this issue, the law calls for not only the government authorities to provide supervision of children to ensure they attend school, but also calls on the townspeople to help support students in their school attendance. As migration from rural to urban areas had increased from the time of the 1986 Compulsory Education

Law, the 2006 law addresses the need to provide for the construction of new schools in newly developed residential areas. The law also makes a provision for county governments to establish boarding schools in areas of need for school-age children living in nonpermanent homes or who are homeless. For teachers, the law reminds them to treat students equally while paying attention to the students' individual differences and abilities.

The law calls for teachers' wages and benefits to be protected and sets expectations that local funding mechanisms for teachers' salaries in rural areas be improved. Salary subsidies, usually used for housing, are provided for special education teachers and teachers in remote and poor areas.

The law reiterates support for teachers' qualifications prescribed by the central government and calls for governments above the county level to strengthen teacher training. The primary effort of this aspect of the law is focused on allocating qualified teachers across the provinces. The law encourages national and local efforts to support urban school teachers and college graduates to move to rural areas to teach.

Expanding Access and Shifting the Curriculum Focus: 2020 National Educational Reform Plan

In 2008, Chinese Premier Wen Jiabao proposed the next generation of a reform program for China's educational system. Premier Wen spent a significant portion of his early career living in the western provinces of China and is sometimes described as having a commoner background. His domestic policies have been described as demonstrating a shift from previous emphases on the growth of the GDP, which would focus investments in large eastern cities to stronger attention to populist concerns across the nation. His education policies illustrate this. In his 2008 speech, Wen said: "Education will take a prominent position as we seek to mitigate the impact of the global financial crisis on our economy. Education has become the cornerstone of national development" (Zhicheng, 2009).

A significant education reform policy followed in 2010 as the National Outline for Medium and Long-term Education Reform and Development (2010–2020), referred to as the 2020 Plan (Link 2-4). This plan was more than a year in development in order to include public consultations, online consultations, and a series of expert roundtables. Both the Minister of Education and the Prime Minister of China participated in its development. The core goals of the 2020 Plan are driven by three primary motivations: (1) address the fallout of the global financial crisis and strengthen China's global and domestic economic position; (2) address the inequities in the school system between rural and border areas and wealthier urban areas; and (3) update and modernize the educational system. These three core drivers of the 2020 Plan are summarized in the opening arguments of the plan:

> In line with the requirements to reach out to modernization, the world and the future, and to meet the demands for building a moderately prosperous society in all respects and an innovative country, it is imperative to regard cultivation of people as a fundamental mission, draw strength from reform and innovation, improve education equity, carry out quality oriented education in an all-round way, push forward scientific education development from a new historical starting point, and speed up the transition from the world's largest education system to one of the world's best, and from a country with large scale of human resource to a country rich in human resources. (p. 6)

The first motivation of the 2020 Plan is around economic development of the country and the increasing economic opportunities for its peoples. According to the 2020 Plan, a core strategy for building the country's economic engine is to invest in the quality of its workforce. Many college graduates could not find employment in the business sectors affected by the recession. At the same time, skilled industrial workers are in high demand in large cities such as Shanghai and Guangdong. The 2020 Plan aims to create stronger vocational programming in rural areas, training millions of migrant workers who are in need of work and who are rapidly moving to industrialized cities. The 2020 Plan emphasizes, "We must cultivate and bring forth quality workers by hundreds of millions, competent professionals by tens of millions, and a large number of top-notch innovative personnel" (p. 8).

The second motivation for the policy is to address inequities within the overall national system of education. Education Minister Yuan Guiren was quoted at an official government meeting in March 2013 as saying, "My dream is to ensure that we can teach students in accordance with their aptitudes, provide education for all people without discrimination, and cultivate every person in this nation to become a talent" (Roberts, 2013). The 2020 Plan acknowledges the disparities within the existing system: " . . . the structure and geographical distribution of education resources are yet to be put on an even keel. Impoverished and ethnic autonomous areas are trailing behind in education development, which is also uneven between urban and rural areas and between different regions" (p. 6). Rural areas are in need of many new resources to build a strong educational system. The number of teachers is inadequate, salaries are low, and facilities are outdated and poorly constructed.

The 2020 Plan addresses these issues of disparity in three ways. First, it proposes to continue to expand the educational system in order to increase the amount of education that people receive. The plan sets strategic enrollment targets for 2020 of universal preschool education, 90% enrollment in senior secondary school, and 40% enrollment rate in higher education. Second, the 2020 Plan makes recommendations for equitable access to education resources by giving preferential access to areas in greatest need:

> Equal access to education is a major cornerstone of social justice. Equal opportunities hold the key to equal access to education. The fundamental requirement of education equity is that all citizens have equal rights to receive education according to law. It is key to boost coordinated development of compulsory education, and to help and support the underprivileged. The fundamental way to achieve this is to allocate education resources reasonably, give preferences to rural, impoverished, remote and border areas and ethnic autonomous areas, and to bridge the gap in education development. (p. 8)

The national government does not propose to take on full responsibility for these increased resources, but encourages provincial and county governments to "guarantee priority to education in local socioeconomic development plans, financial arrangements, and public resource allocation" (p. 7). Additionally, the private sector is called on to "run schools and expand the input of social resources in education" (p. 7). Third, the plan proposes to improve the quality of teaching in rural areas, especially in the primary, junior secondary, and vocational school areas. For example, the plan calls for reform that will attract and keep well-qualified teachers:

> Frameworks and policies shall be adopted to better attract more outstanding professionals to teach in schools. Free education for normal university students shall be advanced. A plan to set up special teaching posts shall be implemented more forcefully to attract teachers to rural schools offering compulsory education. Workable compensation mechanisms shall be endorsed to encourage college graduates to teach in remote areas. The teachers' training system shall be improved, with funding pledged in government budgets. All teachers shall undergo training every five years. The bilingual teachers training must be strengthened in minority-inhabited areas. (p. 37)

The third motivation of the 2020 Plan is on improving the quality of existing educational practices. While the Chinese education system is being hailed for the performance of students in Shanghai and Hong Kong on international exams, there are many aspects of the system that Chinese policy makers, families, and students would like to see improved. The 2020 Plan summarizes the issues: "Our concept of education and our teaching contents and methodology are relatively outdated, school-work burdens on primary and middle school students are too heavy, the promotion of quality education arrested, our students are weak in their adaptability to society, and innovative, practical and versatile professionals is in acute shortage" (p. 6). The 2020 Plan proposes to address these concerns by calling for more student-oriented approaches to teaching; updating the school curriculum in order to allow students to address authentic, real-world problems; promoting less focus on examination preparation; reducing the homework burden on students which creates stress and sleep deprivation; and engaging students in more creative and self-regulated activities. This call for a shift in curricular focus has been characterized as China's efforts to shift away from examination-driven schooling to supporting students in developing creativity and innovative thinking—a shift that requires deep cultural change in how success is viewed and understood by students and their families.

Overall, within this national policy landscape, we see China establish a national nine-year compulsory schooling system that provides access to basic education to everyone. The impact of this policy has been dramatic increases in literacy rates and increasing participation in senior secondary schools across the nation. We also see China make efforts to improve the quality and access of its education systems through systems of teacher training and certification, curriculum reforms, and deepening the local commitment to financing schools. The impact has been a steady increase in national investment in education with targeted programs to support the lesser developed areas of the nation. Curriculum has also undergone much change with lessons designed to be more interactive and local interests integrated into the classroom materials. This will be discussed in more detail in later sections as will a more in-depth discussion of policies and practices that support teacher development.

NOTES

1. All quotes used within the discussion of the national policies are taken directly from the English translations of the national laws and regulations which can be found on the Ministry of Education website and the Database of Laws and Regulations of the PRC government. When page numbers are available in the policy documents, they are provided. See the reference section for the URLs of these websites.

3

CHINA'S EDUCATIONAL SYSTEM TODAY

THIS CHAPTER DESCRIBES THE STRUCTURE of the school system in China today, the governance of the education system, and a description of the nation's teaching population. This context provides a high-level look at how the Chinese schooling system is organized and governed and a broad overview of the population of teachers in China. This section should help the reader position Shanghai's schools within the national schooling design scheme, understand the role of the Ministry of Education in providing policy guidance and program review for Shanghai's provincial education system, and see Shanghai's teaching population within the overall national support for teaches.

The immense population of China is sometimes incomprehensible to those outside of the country. The national education system enrolls more than 200 million K–12 students—two-thirds of the entire US population—in 478,000 elementary and secondary schools (United Nations Children's Fund, 2014). In 2003, China passed a law for the *Promotion of Privately-run Schools* (Database of laws and regulations— China) and private education has been increasing since. The majority of schools in China still identify as public institutions, with less than 10% of the students enrolled in private schools (Simon, 2015). Teacher regulations are nationally established and regardless of whether the school identifies as public or private, schools must hire teachers who meet the national certification expectations (Gang & Meilu, 2007).

The Chinese education system is comprehensive from preschool through adult learning opportunities. The P–12 education system in China comprises three to four years of optional early childhood education, nine years of free, compulsory school split between six years of primary school and three years of junior secondary school, three years of optional senior secondary schooling with options across several tracks

Figure 3.1 China's academic education system.

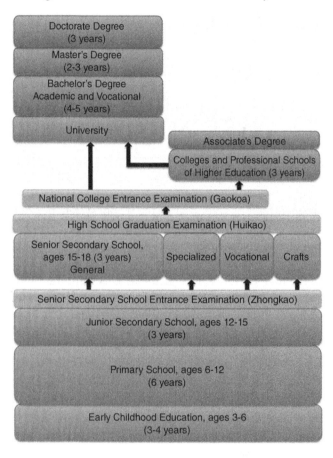

Image from Center for International
Education Bookmarking.

including academic, vocational, and other specialized areas as shown in
Figure 3.1.

The academic year in China runs on a two-semester system, with fall
semester beginning in early September and spring semester beginning
after Spring Festival (Chinese New Year on the Lunar Calendar), usually
in February or March, depending on the lunar calendar. Summer break
usually includes most of July and August. Schools are formally in session
five days a week. Primary schools are typically in session for 38 weeks of
the year, junior secondary schools are in session for 39 weeks, and senior
secondary schools are in session for 40 weeks. The school year activities

typically include 34–36 weeks of class sessions, one week for school activities, one week for community activities, and two weeks for general review and examinations (UNESCO, 2011). In addition to the formal schooling schedule, many children participate in additional after-school educational programs and tutoring sessions at their families' discretion.

Examinations at the elementary school are locally set and are typically required in Chinese and mathematics, the two subjects that receive the most emphasis in the school curriculum. There is no longer an examination entrance requirement for junior secondary school. Placement into senior secondary tracks is determined by student's scores on the entrance *zhongkao* exam and the family ability to pay school fees. Top-performing students will frequently be fully subsidized to attend a school of their choice while others will pay fees that vary based on the student's performance on the entrance exams. In 2012, the gross enrollment rate for secondary school was 89% with 44.5% of those students enrolled in vocational or technical schools (UNESCO, 2014). Some students may not attend senior secondary school due to the cost of attending or in order to work to support their family. The tuition fees for senior secondary school in China vary by region, but generally families pay a few thousand Yuan (or several hundred USD) per year.

Entrance to higher education depends on the student's performance on the *gaokao* exam. Students select their top college or university choices as well as their intended area of study. They will be admitted to one of their choice schools only if they reach that school's cut-off score on the *gaokao* exam.

Governance of the National Education System

Ultimate responsibility for the education system in China lies with the Ministry of Education (MOE). Located in the capital city Beijing, the MOE is an agency of the State Council with the oversight authority for the implementation of national laws and regulations related to the educational system in Mainland China. According to the MOE website, the MOE oversees regulations related to educational reform and development at all levels of the educational system including early childhood education, the nine-year compulsory "basic education," secondary education, vocational education, and tertiary education, which includes colleges, universities, parent education, and other adult education opportunities. The MOE is charged with providing coordination across these different levels of the education system and across different levels of governance and implementation, with attention to equitable distribution of educational resources into ethnic minority areas. The MOE has overall management responsibility for the national education funds and supports local governments in their ability to raise local funds. The MOE also monitors and evaluates the implementation of education directives and programs by providing statistics, analysis, and other research information.

The MOE also creates and approves standardized curriculum catalogues and approves textbooks and teaching materials. This includes ensuring that schools include curriculum in ideology and political education, moral, physical, health, arts, and practical work. One of the many missions of the MOE is to promote the nationwide standardization of the spoken and written Chinese language, including the training of teachers in Putonghua, the standard spoken language of Chinese. Examinations that are regulated nationally are the responsibility of the MOE.

With regard to teachers, the MOE sets the qualification standards and certification exams and establishes requirements for training.

For higher education, the MOE approves all programs, monitors student enrollment, and is responsible for the implementation of the system of conferral of academic degrees. The MOE works with higher education to facilitate graduates' job hunting and starting of their own businesses. Higher education is also expected to support the development of national innovations and State's key projects, with particular attention to the development of science and technology. Higher education is also responsible for supporting MOE initiatives in education related to both teaching and research.

While the MOE of the PRC does not regulate or govern the education systems of Macao, Hong Kong, and Taiwan, the MOE is responsible for educational cooperation and exchanges with these regions. The MOE also promotes international educational exchanges and cooperation including programs for Chinese students studying abroad, foreign students studying in China, joint educational programs by Chinese and foreign educational institutions, managing schools for the children of foreign nationals, and liaising between the State departments and UNESCO. Toward the goals of international relationships, the MOE is also charged to promote the Chinese language across the globe.

Currently, the MOE comprises 21 departments and offices and is affiliated with 34 additional organizations. The Department of Basic Education is the division that oversees all matters related to curriculum development, textbook production, pedagogy enhancement, and school management. The Department of Teacher Education oversees and regulates teacher education programs and the certification exams for teachers. Other departments provide regulations and programming for early childhood education, higher education in colleges and universities, and adult education.

Departmental structure of the PRC's Ministry of Education

○ General Office
○ Department of Policies and Regulations
○ Department of Development and Planning
○ Department of Personnel
○ Department of Finance
○ Department of Basic Education I
○ Department of Basic Education II
○ Department of Vocational and Adult Education
○ Department of Higher Education
○ Office of National Education Inspectorate
○ Department of Ethnic Minority Education
○ Department of Teacher Education
○ Department of Physical, Health and Arts Education
○ Department of Moral Education
○ Department of Social Sciences
○ Department of Science and Technology
○ Department of College Student Affairs
○ Department of National Universities
○ Department of Postgraduate Education (Office of the State Council Academic Degrees Committee)
○ Department of Language Planning and Administration
○ Department of Language Information Management
○ Department of International Cooperation and Exchanges (Office of Hong Kong, Macao and Taiwan Affairs)

http://www.moe.edu.cn/publicfiles/business/htmlfiles/moe/moe_2798/200906/48874.html

The National Education Inspectorate is the agency that monitors and assesses educational activities and the work of primary and secondary schools. The National Inspectorate office hires inspectors from local provinces and liaises with local governments departments of inspection. "The main responsibilities of the departments of inspection at all levels are to: monitor and examine the implementation of State laws, regulations, principles and policies on the part of the governments at the lower level, their departments of education and schools; assess and give guidance to educational work as administered by the governments at the lower level; give advice and report to governments and their education departments with regard to educational activities" (UNESCO, 2011).

The Teaching Population in China

In 2013, China had over 12 million full-time teachers, with just over 7 million pre-primary and primary teachers and 5 million junior and senior secondary teachers (United Nations Children's Fund, 2014). The distribution of teachers across the nation is illustrated in Figure 3.2 (Gang, 2010). Townships and rural areas typically do not sponsor high schools locally and students attend county-level high school instead.

As a nation, China experiences a shortage in qualified teachers that is considered severe in some locations. This is especially true in the rural areas where salaries are lower and working conditions are harsher due to limited school supplies, long distances between towns and other schools, and the general quality of life in poorer economic areas. The national government has instituted some programs to help address the shortages

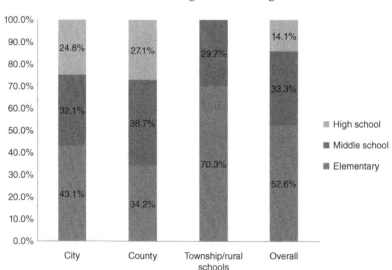

Figure 3.2 Distribution of teachers at different levels of schooling in various regions

Gang, 2010, p. 10, Figure 2.

in rural areas. Since 1997, teacher candidates have had early admission priority at participating universities. This program was based on the logic that the priority admission would attract higher academically performing students into the normal university teaching programs since they would be guaranteed a place at the university with less competition. This does result in some candidates choosing teaching as a career when they would not have done so otherwise in order to secure a place in a university. There is no national data available to attest to whether the quality of the teaching candidate pool has changed due to this program.

Additionally, some of the normal universities were selected to receive funds from the Ministry of Education for scholarship programs for students studying education and seeking their teaching certification. In Shanghai, both East China Normal University and Shanghai Normal University run scholarship programs of this nature. The students selected for this scholarship program (based on competitive exam scores) must return to their home province to teach. Finally, since 1985 graduates from non-normal colleges and universities have been encouraged by the national government to become teachers and have been allowed to teach in public schools (Zhu & Han, 2006). This encouragement continues in current Chinese national policy reform (2020 Plan).

Other programs are aimed at bringing more highly qualified teachers directly into rural China schools. A program offered by the Ministry of Education since 2004 is based on the national "Plans for Nurturing Master of Education for Secondary Schools in Rural Areas." College graduates pursue postgraduate study to become teachers in rural schools. In a five-year cycle the candidate begins teaching in a secondary school in a rural area, then applies for full-time course work at a university in the second year, then completes his or her masters' research paper and oral examination in the third year. They then return to the school where they began in the first year and teach full time in the fourth and fifth years of the program. In 2015, the Rural Teacher Support Program was announced by the State Council. The program will provide more resources such as salary, positions, titles, and in-service training to rural teachers.

Given the national policy context and the description of China's current education system that has been described so far, the next chapter shifts to a discussion of Shanghai and its education system. It is important to remember that Shanghai, while having a reputation of innovation and being ahead of the curve for the reforms that have been supported by the Chinese government, is also responsive to the national policies described earlier.

4

EDUCATION IN SHANGHAI

AS CHINA'S—AND THE WORLD'S—most populous city, Shanghai is one of the most economically advanced metropolitan areas of China. Shanghai has been a source of information and inspiration for national policy in China. At the same time, it operates as a part of the provincial system of education governance and follows the same regulations as the rest of China. Shanghai's system may have benefited by the fact that it is one of four province-level municipalities in China. This means that, as a city, Shanghai has the jurisdictional responsibilities of a province, which allows it to create a unified policy system for managing education and other municipal/provincial responsibilities. Yin Jie, deputy director of Shanghai Municipal Education Commission also has a view toward Shanghai's role in the global education spotlight:

> Education has played an important role in Shanghai and we want Shanghai to be an international mover and shaker in education . . . Since our youths are faced with challenges from around the world, we also hope they can get world-class education in Shanghai and gain the ability to compete on the global stage.
>
> (Shanghai Municipal Information Office, 2012)

Geography and History of the City

Shanghai covers 6,340.5 square kilometers (2,448.1 square miles, or about the size of the state of Delaware in the United States). However, its population of 24 million people is almost the equivalent to that of the state of Texas. Shanghai sits at the mouth of the Yangtze River on the center of China's eastern coastline. This location makes Shanghai a strategic transportation hub with one of the busiest container ports in the world. The city is also split by the Huangpu River.

Figure 4.1 16 districts and 1 county make up the
province-level municipality of Shanghai.

Image from http://www.shanghai.gov.cn/shanghai/node
17256/node17895/index2.html.

Shanghai is divided into 17 county-level divisions referred to
within the city as 16 districts and one county (see Figure 4.1). In addition to the 8 districts that comprise the historic urban core of the city
on the west bank of the Huangpu River, referred to as "Shanghai
proper," there is a newly developed financial district, and 7 additional
districts in suburbs, satellite towns, and rural areas. These outlying districts are still densely populated, with an overall city density of 3,809
people per square kilometer, making Shanghai the most densely populated city in the world (Shanghai Municipal Statistics Bureau, 2015). The
17th district of Shanghai is an island at the mouth of the Yangtze, with a
population density of 500 people per square kilometer.

Shanghai is considered one of China's key economic engines with a diverse array of industry from retail and IT to transportation and finance. In summary:

> Shanghai plays an important role in the nations' social and economic development as the international metropolis-oriented city is striving to serve the nation and lead the growth of the Yangtze River Delta region. With only 0.06% of the nation's land area, Shanghai contributes 4.2% of China's GDP. The volume of cargo handled at local ports accounts for 8.1% of the nations' total, and the value of imports and exports accounts for 12.4% of the nation's total.
>
> (Shanghai Municipal Statistics Bureau, 2011, p. 15)

As a global financial center, Shanghai is often viewed as the trendsetting city for Chinese policy and practice. Some trace this quality of Shanghai to its 19th-century history of being divided into "concessions" among several Western nations. These land areas within the city were like small colonies of Great Britain, France, and the United States. International business leaders brought an entrepreneurial and market-driven element into the city's industry and development. In its 20th-century development, Shanghai is viewed as the first city to economically and educationally "recover" from the Cultural Revolution by rebuilding schools and leading China's early effort to advance market enterprises in the nation's overall move toward a "socialist market economy" (Cheng & Yip, 2006).

By the dawn of the 21st century, Shanghai had become the strongest local economy in Mainland China, with a total GDP of 1.92 trillion Yuan ($297 billion USD) and a per capita GDP of 82,560 Yuan ($12,784 USD) in 2011. In 2013 China announced an experimental "free trade zone" in an 11-square-mile area of Shanghai illustrating how Shanghai continues to be a testing ground for national economic reforms trending toward market approaches. In sum, Shanghainese live within the strong cultural traditions of China, and at the same time, Shanghai vies with Hong Kong for the moniker of the "most global city in China" in the context of globalization.

Shanghai's Schools and Students

Shanghai's public education system supports 1.5 million students in 759 primary schools, 762 regular junior and senior secondary schools, and 103 specialized secondary education schools. In addition, almost 300 nonpublic schools (primary, junior, and senior secondary) operate in the city. Shanghai is also the home of 68 public higher education institutions (Shanghai Statistical Yearbook, 2014).

In 2010, all school-age children in Shanghai attended nine-year compulsory education, including all of the children living with parents who are migrant workers (Shanghai Municipal Statistics Bureau, 2011). Shanghai was the first province in China to achieve 100% elementary and junior secondary school enrollment and, today, has achieved almost universal secondary school attendance, even among its migrant student population (OECD, 2010). Access to higher education has also opened up dramatically for students in Shanghai. In 2004, 75% of secondary graduates continued to higher education with 45% attending universities and 30% attending other types of postsecondary education (Cheng & Yip, 2006).

Shanghai's more than 24 million people include permanent residents who hold *hukou* status within the city and migrants who have settled in the city. The *hukou* is a national system of household registration for families based on their permanent residence or land ownership. Within this system, families register in their home provinces, and while they may migrate to other parts of the country, their permanent residence is identified in the province where they are registered. A family's *hukou* status determines their access to social systems such as health care, education, welfare, and housing opportunities. A child's *hukou* is determined by his or her parents' *hukou* and not the child's birthplace. If parents do not share the same *hukou*, the child can choose between the two.

While the *hukou* system dates back to ancient times, in modern times it became more strictly enforced in the 1950s, during Mao Zedong's rule, as a way to limit and control the rural population's movement into the cities during times of famine and abject poverty. It serves a similar population migration control purpose today along with providing a mechanism for record keeping of births, deaths, marriages, and relocations. The *hukou* continues to limit migrants' access to social benefits and programs, including schooling, within the urban centers and creates a two-tiered population status within cities. Shanghai's recent efforts to close the opportunity gap with respect to migrant children's education are described in a later section.

The *hukou* classifies individuals into two categories—urban or rural. Based on 2010 census numbers, Shanghai's population was 89% urban and 11% rural (World Population Review). With its increasing industrial and commercial growth, Shanghai not only attracts migrant workers from across the nation, its economy depends on this work force given that Shanghai has reported a negative population growth rate among its permanent residents since 1993 (Shanghai Municipal Statistics Bureau, 2011). The city population continues to grow due to an influx of migrants from other parts of the country.

Meeting the Needs of Migrant Children in Shanghai's Schools

In 2014 Shanghai was the home of more than 14 million migrant people (Shanghai Municipal Statistics Bureau, 2015). Roughly 20% of the entire student population at the basic education level in Shanghai are children of migrant families (OECD, 2011, p. 96). As migrant workers move to the eastern and southern cities, the recipient cities are challenged by the cost of educating large populations of children of families that were not contributing to the local tax base. Resident parents in the cities also balked at the idea of mixing migrant children into the local school population for fear of decreasing the quality of their own children's education. Critics of China's, and particularly Shanghai's, approach to the schooling of migrant children identify three key areas of neglect for migrant children's education by pointing to (1) the inferior quality of migrant children schools; (2) the limitations on access to a public school; and (3) the high mobility of migrant students (Wang & Holland, 2011).

At the core of the criticism of Shanghai's treatment of migrant children is the *hukou* system. A 2002 national policy made an effort to clarify where the responsibility for educating migrant children lay: "Education of migrant children is mainly the responsibility of the recipient city," and "migrant children should be educated mainly in public schools" (OECD, p. 96). However, when migrant children do not have a *hukou* in the city where their family is currently living, they are frequently required to enroll in private schools that have been established specifically for migrant children. Families pay tuition for private schools. Tuition and fees vary across the private schools, running between 500–800 Yuan per semester ($85–133 USD) with some schools granting waivers, reductions, or providing payment plans.

Many of these private schools receive indirect funding from the national government by being registered as a school serving a province where its migrant population is from, yet they are not fully funded by the local school district because they are in a limbo state between public funded schools and schools viewed as a private school by the local government. Often, these schools can be left unmonitored by the local government, have inferior physical space and supplies in comparison to the public schools, and many have lower teaching quality based on teacher qualifications and reports from parents and students (Wang & Holland, 2011).

Shanghai established that migrant children are "our children" and has made efforts to ensure a quality education experience for children of migrant families (OECD, 2011, p. 96). The Municipal Education Commission is making an effort to reduce the number of schools designated as private schools for migrant children and enroll them in regular public schools. Specific public schools are now designated within districts for migrant children.

Enrollment in a public school is not without its barriers, including overburden of documentation to ensure enrollment, segregation within schools, and fees. The families must be able to provide a certificate of immunization, household registration for student and parents, a certificate attesting to the fact that the student is a single child, temporary residence permits for both parents, and an apartment lease within the district of application (Wang & Holland, 2011). In some of the designated public schools for migrant children the students face segregation practices by being placed in specialized classes for migrant children (Wang & Holland, 2011). Since 2009 Shanghai public schools are not supposed to charge tuition or fees to migrant families for public school enrollment in the compulsory grades.

All children of migrant families also face the problem of attending senior secondary school. Compulsory education ends at grade nine, or about age 14. To attend senior secondary school and take the college entrance exams, migrant children have to return to their place of household registration. Attending high school in Shanghai requires migrant children to pass selection exams and pay higher fees than they would if they attended high school in their town of *hukou* residency.

Controversy about Migrant Children and the PISA Exam Results

The controversy over the *hukou* system and its impact on migrant children was prominently discussed among education leaders and reformers with the release of Shanghai's performance on the PISA exams. Accusations of sampling students from elite schools and eliminating the migrant student populations from the sample have been leveled by Tom Loveless, a senior research fellow at the Brookings Institution in Washington, D.C (Loveless, 2013) and Professor Kam Wing Chan at the University of Washington (Gao, 2014). For both Loveless and Chan, the exclusion of migrant children from the Shanghai PISA sample is linked to the Chinese *hukou* system and the return of these children to their home provinces to attend high school.

Figure 4.2 The migration pattern for children in Shanghai shows a steady decline, reaching a low point at age 14, just before the PISA sample age of 15, when the numbers begin to increase after children have completed their nine years of compulsory education.

Educational migration

China's household registration system, known as the hukou system, ties access to subsidized education and health care to hometowns. As a result, many of Shanghai's migrant children return home until they complete middle school, after which many return to Shanghai for jobs.

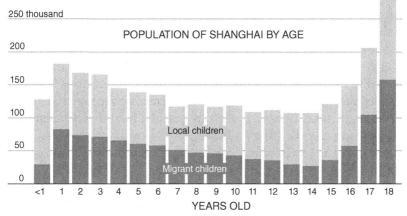

Sources: Kam Wing Chan, Professor in the Department of Geography at the University of Washington, based on the Shanghai Population Census 2010, Volumes 1 and 3

According to Chan's data (Figure 4.2) "the percentage of migrant children out of the total child population in Shanghai declines steadily in each age bracket starting at age 8. It picks up again at the age of 16, as migrants, having completed middle school in their home provinces, swarm to Shanghai seeking jobs" (Gao, 2013). Based on this data, the PISA sample of 15-year-olds will access fewer migrant children in the 15-year-old age bracket of the testing sample. Chan also reports that the migrant children who are left in the Shanghai educational system are from more affluent or better-educated families.

OECD and Shanghai officials stand by their sampling procedures of students within Shanghai as following the OECD protocols and maintain that the sample is representative of the population of students in Shanghai schools. Zhang Minxuan, former president of Shanghai Normal University and the Shanghai coordinator for PISA, reported that "the

proportion of 'new Shanghai residents' [how migrant students were classified in the PISA sample] in the pool of all PISA students accounted for
19.8 percent in 2009 and increased to 26.5 percent in 2012. This number
is very close to 27.73 percent from the national population census representing the proportion of residents without Shanghai *hukou*" (Zhang,
2013).

OECD PISA developer Schleicher also points out the overall strength
of the Shanghai student performance by making comparisons to the
highest performing students in the United States: "There are limitations
in the ways we conducted the test in most countries, . . . but even when
you exclude the 30 percent of worst-performing students in the United
States, Shanghai still performs No. 1" (Gao, 2014).

Another approach to comparing Shanghai student performance to
other nations is to look at the performance of the lowest performing
students in the Shanghai sample. The bottom quartile of students in the
Shanghai sample scored a mean of 562 points on the mathematics exam.
The OECD mean score for the bottom quartile of students is 452. The
lowest performing Shanghai students performed better than the highest
performing students (those in the top quartile) in all but 10 countries.
Only the top quartile students in Belgium, Germany, Korea, the Neth-
erlands, Poland, Switzerland, Hong Kong, Liechtenstein, Singapore,
and Thailand scored more than 562 points on average (OECD, 2014c,
p. 185, Table II.2.4a).

OECD also reports on the performance of "resilient" students. Resil-
ience is defined as if a student "is in the bottom quarter of the PISA index
of economic, social and cultural status (ESCS) in the country/economy
of assessment and performs in the top quarter of students from all coun-
tries/economies, after accounting for socio-economic status" (OECD,
2014c, p. 194). Within Shanghai's sample, 19.2% of the students were
classified as resilient, the highest percentage recorded for all jurisdictions in the sample (OECD, 2014c, p.185, Table II.2.7a). The OECD
mean percentage for resilient students was 6.4%. While the national and
provincial governments continue to work on policies that make public
resources more available to migrant families across China, it appears,
based on these PISA data, that Shanghai has made inroads into educating
students from lower socioeconomic backgrounds that results in a strong
performance on this measure of achievement.

The controversy surrounding the PISA results with regard to the
hukou system has raised awareness and critique around the world about
this residential registration system in China. Shanghai officials are aware
of the effect of the *hukou* on Shanghai students. Yin Houqing, former

deputy director of the Shanghai Municipal Education Commission, was reported as saying, "We need to create conditions, strengthen the system's design, and coordinate the interests of all parties, steadily going forward in an orderly manner to allow more migrant worker children to attend urban high schools and universities...We must consider the interests of migrant children, but at the same time we must take into account the impact on the capacity and sustainable development of our urban resources" (Roberts, 2013).

In 2013, China began instituting reforms in how workers from other provinces register within cities and become eligible for services and benefits, using Shanghai as a testing ground. The pilot program in Shanghai uses a point system based on the migrant's economic, social, and educational status. For example, points are awarded for factors such as already possessing a college degree (and sometimes this is restricted to particular in-demand areas such as the sciences), owning a business or property, or earning a salary that meets a threshold. If the applicant meets a threshold number of points, he or she is granted a local Shanghai residence permit and the resident's family becomes eligible for city and national benefits within their new provincial residence.

In July 2014, vice public security minister Huang Ming reported that the government would further reform the national *hukou* system by removing the limits on *hukou* registration in townships and small cities, relaxing restrictions in medium-sized cities (with populations between 1 and 3 million), and setting qualifications for registration in big cities (over 5 million residents) by developing a point system based on factors such as seniority in employment, living accommodation, and social security similar to the system piloted in Shanghai (Zhang, 2014).

Governance of the Shanghai Education System

Governments at the provincial, municipal, and county levels each have Education Commissions responsible for the administration of education programs and compliance with national laws and regulations. The regional Education Commissions make local implementation decisions about regional development plans, provide local funds to subsidize national funding, make curriculum choices with approval from the national level, provide professional development and training for teachers, and administer school programs. The Shanghai Municipal Education Commission (Link 4-1) is the leading governing body for ensuring compliance with national laws and setting provincial-specific policy in Shanghai. The Commission supports several bureaus to ensure that the system has the necessary resources and holds the entire system accountable. The Shanghai educational system is held accountable for all of the national laws and regulations and, in many instances, Shanghai is used as a testing ground for rolling out the implementation of new national educational policies much like it is for experimenting with new economic models.

At the school level, principals oversee the staffing needs of the school, set class sizes and teacher assignments, and ensure that the physical plant of the school is operational. Principals evaluate teachers and set the procedures for merit pay for teachers. Principals can also identify special needs of a school and apply for additional funding from the provincial Education Commission to meet those needs. With regard to participation in educational decision making, teachers develop their own lesson plans and serve on advisory groups established by the principal.

Education Financing in Shanghai

In Spring 2012, the Shanghai municipal government planned to invest 70 billion Yuan (approximately $11.6 billion USD) in its education system the following year. About 67% of those funds were directed to the districts and the remaining third was kept at the municipal level. Overall, 68% (47.3 billion Yuan; $7.8 billion USD) was directed to compulsory and preschool education; 25% (17.7 billion Yuan; $3 billion USD) was directed to higher education; and the remaining 7% (4.97 billion Yuan; $833 million USD) was directed to vocational training (Shanghai Municipal Information Office, 2012).

One of Shanghai's recent initiatives is to reconfigure its district-to-school financing systems, creating a financial transfer payment as a mechanism to mobilize public funds differently. Accompanying this plan is an effort to provide greater access to schooling for migrant children within the city. The director of the Municipal Education Commission, Xue Mingyang, reported that:

> In compulsory education, we will make great efforts to improve school facilities in suburban and rural areas. Each new town or large-scale residential community will have their share of schools and many existing school buildings will be reinforced and renovated. We will also subsidize privately-run schools for children of migrant workers and encourage experienced teachers to work in suburban schools. To achieve these, we need to reform the fund allocation mechanism and establish a public online platform to facilitate fund distribution. We also need to improve the fund use efficiency at the district level. The usage of education funds will be supervised by

the Municipal Government Education Supervision Office and all information will be made public according to relevant rules. We also welcome the supervision of the entire society, including news media.

(Shanghai Municipal Information Office, 2012)

Chen and Feng (2012) report that while the quality of privately run schools for migrant children is generally much worse than the publicly funded schools in Shanghai, the municipal government has come through with increased funding through annual subsidies and stronger government oversight of these schools. The result is that student performance in these schools is on the rise and parent satisfaction with schools has improved. Interviews with school principals and teachers suggest that the increased government funds for the schools has provided better physical conditions within the schools, greater stability among the teaching staff, and higher quality teaching (Chen & Feng, 2012).

Family Commitment to Education in Shanghai

There is no question that parents invest heavily in their child's education from elementary grades on. During a child's elementary school years, Shanghai parents annually spend, on average, 6,000 Yuan ($960 USD) on English and math tutors and 9,600 Yuan ($1500 USD) on weekend activities such as sports and music lessons (Jiang, 2011). During the high school years, annual tutoring costs can rise dramatically to 30,000 Yuan ($4800 USD) and the cost of activities doubles to 19,200 Yuan ($3000 USD) (Jiang, 2011).

When interviewing principals for her research on the Shanghai education system, Tan (2013) reported that when she asked them what they thought the main factors contributing to the Shanghai students' success on PISA was, parental support and commitment was always part of their response. One principal said: "Parents devote money, time and energy to their child's education . . . As long as the child is willing to learn, more than 95% of parents are willing to spend the money, even if 70% of family expenses go to the child's learning" (p. 53).

In the spirit of Shanghai's global presence, some journalists report that "Shanghai parents are giving their children the best of both education worlds: a Shanghai kindergarten to grade 12 education and a US higher education" (Jiang, 2011). Shanghai students are increasingly planning to and are attending US colleges and universities. In 2005, 110,000 Shanghai students participated in the *gaokao* exam for college entrance within China. By 2011, that number dwindled to 61,000 as Shanghainese students chose to study abroad for college. This decline may also be mitigated by the ongoing decline of the Shanghai-born population as noted earlier. By comparison, in Yunnan Province, where most families cannot afford to study overseas, students participating in the *gaokao* increased from 170,000 in 2005 to 220,000 in 2010. Most Shanghainese students who have studied abroad are expected to return to Shanghai and contribute to its growing economy (Jiang, 2011).

Educational Reform Efforts in Shanghai

Shanghai's educational reforms over the past 30 years align with the national government's efforts to improve education through its policies. Shanghai is often used as a testing ground for new national policies. Vivian Stewart, senior advisor for education and former vice president of the Asia Society, describes Shanghai's educational reform in broad strokes over time:

> It is not something that happened overnight. It was a 30-year process of gradual improvement. In the 70s and 80s, the push was about expanding access to schools. In the 90s the focus shifted to improving the quality. A national curriculum reform effort was piloted in Shanghai, and later spread around the country, to broaden the curriculum beyond math and science to arts and literature and also to initiate change towards more active kinds of pedagogy. There was also a major emphasis on upgrading the teaching force and trying to reduce examination pressure. In Shanghai, we abolished end of primary school exams, so schools could focus on deeper learning rather than teaching to the exams.

> In the 1990s, in the big cities, there were "key" High Schools that had very high standards. At those schools, 15-year-old Chinese students could talk to you in English about the science experiments or extra-curricular club they were engaged in or about American history or geography and current affairs. But there was a big gap between these key schools and other schools. So in Shanghai as well as in some other eastern cities, they decided they had to bring up the bottom schools, which included large numbers of poor students whose families had migrated to the cities from the countryside. Shanghai experimented with lots of ways to bring up the bottom.

> (Tucker, 2014, p. 9)

We can see in this narrative of reform that the national policies since 1986 had significant consequences for the Shanghai education system and Shanghai has led the country in creating approaches to meeting the expectations of those laws and national reform plans. In this section, I will examine three efforts at educational reform in Shanghai—curriculum and teaching reform, approaches to improving the overall quality schools, and addressing the needs of migrant children.

Reforms in Curriculum and Teaching

Curricular reforms over time have given new shape to what and how students learn in Shanghai schools. In the 1980s, elective courses were introduced into the curriculum. After the 1995 Education Law went into effect, curriculum approaches began integrating the sciences with the humanities and more emphasis was placed on active inquiry. During the post-2006 policy reforms, schools are still working to reshape teaching and learning to give students more opportunity "to learn to learn" and not just learn the curriculum content. These curriculum reform efforts reflect efforts to include independent learning opportunities that support more creative thinking.

Shanghai has been making strong efforts to reform the basic classroom pedagogy in schools. Teachers are encouraged to allow time for student activities in classrooms rather than relying solely on presentations and lectures. The municipal slogan is "return class time to students" (OECD, 2010, p. 4). There is also an effort to make classroom learning more problem-centered to allow students opportunities to think critically. Here, the slogan is "to every question there should be more than a single answer" (OECD, 2010, p. 4). For example, I observed a mathematics lesson for fifth graders at Qilun Primary School in Shanghai taught by a teacher in her second year of teaching. This lesson was conducted as a demonstration lesson, with 12 observers including myself, three principals and five teachers from another district, and three people from East China Normal University Institute for Schooling Reform and Development. The students were given a small pouch containing geometric shapes such as squares, triangles, rectangles, and parallelograms and some short sticks. The lesson was focused on how lines and angles create polygons and the characteristics of these polygons.

The teacher led the students through the 35-minute lesson at a rapid pace, introducing the students to the activity and then asking them to use the manipulatives to explore relationships among the shapes. The students worked individually and talked in pairs. The teacher then called the whole class back together to talk about the students' observations. She prompted them to focus on the relationship of the sides and angles within parallelograms using the small sticks among the materials the students had at their desks. The class ended with a discussion of where parallelograms are seen and used in everyday life.

This lesson engaged the students in an exploration of what they already knew or could derive from their initial observations using the materials, introduced the new shape of parallelogram, and allowed students to explore the relationship among lines and angles that create parallelograms. The lesson discussion among teachers that followed the classroom instruction highlighted the importance of giving students the opportunity to work on a task that challenged them to use the information they had already learned—for example, what they learned about squares and triangles in earlier grades—while also allowing them to form habits of how to explore new ideas and new understandings. The focus on how to best engage the students in their own desktop activity toward grasping the concepts within the lesson were central to the discussion of the teachers and principals in the lesson discussion meeting.

The current curriculum has three parts: (1) basic curriculum, experienced by all students, implemented through compulsory courses; (2) enriched curriculum aimed at developing students' potential offered through elective courses; (3) inquiry-based curriculum implemented primarily through extracurricular activities outside of the regular school schedule with support and guidance from teachers. In these programs, students identify research topics based on their interests and pursue independent projects. The enrichment programs, however, still compete with the demands of the *zhongkao* (the senior secondary school placement exam) and the *gaokao* (the college placement exam), so these courses and programs tend to be short term and placed early in the students' school career. Shanghai also began transforming the city-administered exams to give them more focus on application to real-life problems and skills and multiple-choice questions were removed from the city's exams.

One might assume that Shanghai has reached its goals for curriculum and instruction reform given the strong performance of its students on the PISA exams, which are designed to measure how students can extract and use information in novel situations. Within Shanghai, however, many officials and education professionals do not consider the PISA exam results to hold much meaning for continued improvement of the Shanghai education system.

Professor Ye Lan of East China Normal University has been working toward school reform in Shanghai for almost two decades (Ye, 2009) and was the founding Director of the Institute of Schooling Reform and Development at the university. Through her research, she knows what students can accomplish when they are guided by engaging pedagogy that allows them to think for themselves and create new ideas. When she discussed the Shanghai PISA results she acknowledged that the results demonstrate that students in Shanghai are motivated learners and are well trained to solve exam questions. But, for Professor Ye, she would rather see students thinking and creating and innovating as an outcome of their education (Ye Lan, interview, 26 November 2013). She thinks the focus inside Shanghai should be more strongly centered on school reform through instructional change. This sentiment was echoed by others. During interviews in this study, teachers and principals acknowledged that they were pleased with the results of Shanghai students on the PISA exams, but they were quick to say that the results showed only that the students were meeting the basic skills of education and that they were striving to improve the students' ability to be problem solvers, flexible thinkers, and to have more happiness and passion in their learning. While being proud of the PISA results, they almost dismissed them as nonconsequential because their current efforts to transform the schooling and learning experience of students are not measured by exams like the PISA assessments.

Improving the Overall Quality of Schools

Shanghai places much of its efforts in educational reform at the school level. Here, I discuss four approaches to school-level reform in Shanghai: improving the physical conditions of schools, removing special designations for elite schools, creating a neighborhood attendance system, and using "empowered management" between low-performing and high-performing schools.

Shanghai has made consistent efforts to improve the physical condition of schools with major renovations in the 1980s and again in the 1990s. In the early 2000s Shanghai introduced a rating system that evaluates the infrastructure as well as the educational quality of the school using a four-level rating: A, B, C, D. Many C and D schools were closed while others were merged into level A or B schools or reorganized. By 2005, level C and D schools no longer existed and all public schools became level A or B (OECD, 2010).

In the late 1980s, Shanghai took bold steps to even the quality of schools across its system by removing special designations of schools as "key schools." This national approach of establishing schools with special funding for experimental programs and high standards of admission was meant to drive improvement in the educational system by allowing specialized programs to develop within these schools and create demonstration sites for how to run "model schools." Key schools were especially important in the 1980s as China was emerging from the Cultural

Revolution in order to set the example for the envisioned future of education in the country. Over time, key schools became very competitive for students to gain admission and they became elite institutions.

Starting in 1994, Shanghai began removing the key school designation in an effort to mitigate the competition for school attendance. Shanghai then introduced a "neighborhood attendance" policy at the primary and junior secondary levels, thus changing the teaching ecology in the city. The national government followed Shanghai's example and abolished the key school designation in the 2006 new Compulsory Education Law. The rationale given within this law is stated earlier: to "narrow the gap" in the quality of schools.

In the neighborhood attendance scheme, students would attend their local schools and not compete to enter key schools. This policy worked against the prevailing culture within families which was to seek the best school for their children regardless of where it was located, and was met with confusion, push back, and disgruntlement. The social pressure was so great that eventually a compromise was reached: students could choose schools in other neighborhoods by paying a "sponsorship fee," creating a new version of a school choice system. With neighborhood attendance, public examinations at the end of primary school were no longer necessary for placement into junior secondary schools. According to the OECD (2010), without the pressure of examinations, primary schools almost immediately became centers of innovation and creativity.

In the past decade, Shanghai has developed an innovative approach to bringing up low-performing schools through its "commissioned education program" or "empowered management" program (Jensen & Farmer, 2013). What was once a focus on identifying a few "key schools" for strong investment is now an effort to raise the overall quality of the system. In this approach school-district leaders match low-performing schools with high-performing schools. The high-performing school is contracted to support and develop the low-performing school in specified areas—for example, teaching quality, school management, relationships within parents. The performance of the low-performing school is carefully monitored through evaluations conducted by the district bureaus. The high-performing school is only contractually paid if the terms of the contract have been met, meaning that the low-performing school is demonstrating some success. The contract can be ended and payments can be withheld if the relationship does not result in improved performance.

Other types of arrangements are also made between schools in efforts toward school improvement. For example, principals from high-performing schools may be asked to manage multiple schools, or schools in geographic proximity with each other can be formed into clusters to share resources, including sharing teachers. Higher education is also engaged in some of these efforts. For example, The Institute for Schooling Reform and Development at East China Normal University supports Minhang District in developing school associations to conduct joint research-based activities aimed at schooling reform.

The empowered management approach to school reform strongly relies on the expertise of its best principals and teachers to reform its failing schools. For the high-performing schools, the opportunity to enter into such contracts brings more prestige to their staff and their schools. The Shanghai government promised career advancement opportunities and autonomy if educators could turn around low-performing schools.

The empowered management approach can happen within the city and also through exchange program with poor rural schools:

> In 2007, the Shanghai municipal government asked 10 good schools in downtown and other educational intermediary agencies to take charge of 20 schools providing compulsory education in 10 rural districts and counties. The good schools/agencies and the rural schools signed a two-year contract that required the former to send senior administrators and experienced teachers to the latter. The city government bears the cost of the partnership (Shanghai Municipal Education Commission, 2008). Such an arrangement not only benefits the poor schools; it also gives the good schools more room to promote their teachers.
>
> (OECD, 2010)

I spent a full day visiting Qibao Experimental Middle School, interviewing school principal, Zha Jian Sheng, and some of the teachers, observing lessons, and a lesson study group meeting. Zha Jian Sheng had been an experienced and award-winning teacher himself in Qibao School, a highly regarded and well-performing school in Shanghai. Shixi Middle School, a school that ranked near the bottom of Shanghai Middle Schools, was taken into the Qibao Education Group, a school management group built around Qibao School. Zha Jian Sheng became the principal of the Experimental School, and the school was renamed Qibao Experimental Middle School. Now, in his fifth year at the school, the school has seen rapid progress in its students' performance.

Zha Jian Sheng attributed much of the school progress to the opportunity to work with a better-performing school. This relationship was primarily described as an opportunity to learn from the better school. These opportunities included having teacher exchanges between the schools.

Principal: We send outstanding young teachers to prestigious schools to learn, for a year, to teach. They send outstanding teachers in their middle ages, lead teachers, to our school for a year. Every year, we send three teachers over and host three teachers from them. We send three young teachers, young and outstanding, while they send us three middle-aged outstanding teachers.

Teacher: Actually we go to their school to learn how to teach and they come to our school to lead us to teach and demonstrate how they teach in prestigious schools.

Principal: They come to our community. Yes, officially assigned teachers.

(Interview, Qibao Experimental Middle School,
14 November 2013)

The schools also maintained communication among groups of teachers for lesson design and planning. On the day of my visit, a teacher from Qibao School was visiting the Experimental School to watch a lesson and participate in the teacher lesson discussion. Finally, Zha Jian Sheng described how master teachers from Qibao School are also matched up with teachers who are particularly weak in the Experimental School in order to serve as mentors and help with improvement.

Zha Jian Sheng attributed his school's success to two areas of focus in their improvement efforts: active and motivating classroom instruction for the students and particular attention to the development of young teachers. As he described teaching practices that are actively engaging, Zha Jian Sheng explicitly drew on what he called both Eastern and Western values. From the Eastern perspective, the students' commitment is to hard work and diligence—a focus on effort as opposed to a focus on inherent ability. In this Eastern mindset, you can be successful if you put the time and effort into the work. From the Western perspective, Zha Jian Sheng spoke of independent learning, cooperation, curiosity, teamwork, and creativity. To illustrate what this looks like in instruction, he made a reference to John Dewy and his ideas of learning from experience.

For the teachers in Qibao Experimental School, shifting instructional practices to ones that engage students in experience and activity was challenging at first. They had to learn new processes of student activity and give more thought to how to build on experience over time. They report today that they find more enjoyment in teaching because the students do not seem bored. They also see the weakest-performing students perform better. Teachers in the interview agreed, if they were to go back to their traditional ways of teaching they and their students "would be miserable."

Finally, Zha Jian Sheng emphasized the importance of investing in his youngest and newest teachers. Through his leadership, the beginning teachers should learn to teach in more active ways from the beginning of their career and not have to relearn how to teach later. He advocated and supported more opportunities for teachers to go out and learn from others, to arrange opportunities for experienced teachers to work with beginning teachers, and to take care of the beginning teachers with special care. The partnerships within the Qibao Education Group allow him to provide these opportunities for his least-experienced teachers. During our day together, he went out of his way to introduce me to some of his brightest star teachers beginning their careers and to praise them for their work in front of his outside visitor. Zha Jian Sheng began and ended our time together with the same idea: "Cultivate a strong team of leaders to help students, teachers, and the school to develop better."

5

TEACHING IN CHINA AND SHANGHAI

IN 1993 CHINA ESTABLISHED an all-encompassing *Teachers Law* (Link 5-1) and declared teaching a "profession," echoing many international education experts who described teaching as work that required a specified body of knowledge, a set of agreed-upon skills, and the ability to make sound judgments during the course of daily interactions with students. With this professional status defined in law, teachers in China must meet specific criteria and pass an exam to acquire a teaching certificate. In addition, teachers in China are expected to embody and explicitly teach students personal health and well-being, the moral tenets that are held within the culture, and the ideological expectations of the People's constitution based on Communist political principles.

The following sections describe the cultural view of teachers within China, the specific expectations for teachers encoded in China's laws, how school structures shape teachers' work, the policies for how teachers are prepared, and a description of the current teaching population and recruitment efforts. In policy, we see a similar pattern for governing teachers' work as we saw in the overall educational system policies—an initial focus on establishing a system with criteria and regulatory controls, a move to ensure quality within the system, and then more focus on equitable distribution of teaching resources nationally.

Teaching within the Chinese Culture

Based on my interviews and reading about teachers and teaching in China, I propose that there are three ways to view and understand how teachers are perceived in China. First, there is a long history of reverence for teachers in the Chinese culture. Teachers in China generally hold special status in relationship with their students and their families. We can see some aspects of this special relationship to teachers in the root of the Chinese word for teaching:

> . . . the Chinese word for "teacher" is "jiaoshi" which comprises two characters: "jiao" which means "teach" and "shi" which means "master" or "expert". Therefore, the term "jiaoshi" underscores the cultural belief that a teacher should not just be an instructor but a "teaching master" or "teaching expert."
>
> (Tan, 2013, p. 34)

Here, the teacher is viewed as an authority on their discipline and one who can guide students successfully through their studies. To become educated is tightly linked to the potential success one has in life. For parents, the success of their children is of core importance, and supporting their child's education is paramount.

Teachers are also viewed as special people in the *lives* of students, not only in their formal education. Teachers are expected to be models for leading a moral lives and their responsibilities to their students go beyond the instructional time in the classroom—teachers frequently meet with students in the teachers' office to provide additional tutoring or assistance with their academic work and to encourage them to improve. Students then view their teachers as part of the fundamental supports for how they live their lives with virtue. This belief is exemplified in the Tao traditions of ritual in which the phrase "Heaven-Earth-Sovereign-Parent-Teacher" is repeated and becomes ingrained in how one sees himself holistically governed and supported.

The teacher is also viewed as an elder with wisdom who enters the students' lives and stays with them. I observed the cultural routines of respect between younger and elder in the classroom. When students answer questions, they stand at their desks; students present their work to the teacher using both hands; and students greet their teachers pleasantly. Teachers are not only part of the school life of the students. As an elder, as someone who invests in the nurturing of youth, the teacher becomes symbolic in the students' lives as a figure who provides guidance that is carried throughout life. This is exemplified in a well-known saying in China: "One day as my teacher, the rest of my life as my father."

The second way to view how teachers are perceived in China is as an occupation—teaching in China is relatively high status work. For example, in surveys of occupational prestige, teaching is ranked above occupations such as corporate managers and mid-level military officers (Li et al., 2004 as cited in Ingersoll, 2007). However, as an occupation, teaching is on par with the work of civil servants as described in the Teachers' Law with regard to their salaries and benefits. This tension between the social status and the salaried status of the occupation creates much policy frustration. There is a desire to improve the status of teachers and attract more people from high status colleges and universities to become teachers through increased salaries, yet local resources for salaries are often not available.

The third way to view teachers in China is that teaching is a stable career that generates a stable salary. In China, competition for jobs is fierce. For a young college graduate, especially for women, securing a position as a school teacher will almost always ensure them a job with a high degree of job security and enough salary to live in reasonable comfort. A group of female teacher candidates from Shanghai Normal University participated in a focus group in the fall of 2013. When asked why they wanted to be a teacher, the first response was, "I love children," and most of the women around the table agreed that this was a motivation for them. A second response also captured much agreement from the group: "My parents think that to be a teacher is very stable work for girls. Maybe all of us will be wives and mothers so we have enough holidays to help our family." A third response supported this stance: "I think teachers' salary is suitable for girls."

Establishing Teaching as a Profession: National Teacher Laws and Regulations in the 1990s

China began efforts to professionalize teaching when it passed the *People's Republic of China Teachers Law* in 1993. This law went into effect in 1994 and was soon followed by the *Regulations for Qualification of Teachers* in 1995 and reinforced with the *Implementation of Regulations for Qualification of Teachers* in 2000. Provinces and schools use the national laws to guide their local decisions about teacher qualifications, teacher salaries, and teacher work assignments.[1]

The 1993 Teachers Law defines teachers as professionals and establishes the expectation that the nation should give attention to the "professional training of teachers, improving teachers' working and living conditions, protecting the legitimate rights and interests of teachers, improving the social status of teachers . . . The whole society should respect teachers." September 10 was established as Teachers' Day—a day to recognize, award, and celebrate teachers across the nation. On Teachers' Day, many award ceremonies are held to recognize accomplished teachers.

In law, the central government authorized schools to manage their teachers, making decisions about employment, teaching assignments, and professional support. In the structure of the policy, teachers are afforded a set of "rights" and a set of "duties." Teachers were given the right to carry out educational reform and experiment, engage in scientific research and academic exchanges, and participate in professional academic organizations and academic activities. The law also gives teachers the right to participate in a "staff congress or other forms of democratic participation in school management." In terms of employment benefits, the law gives teachers the right to "obtain wages, benefits and enjoy the state's summer and winter holidays paid leave."

The law also establishes clear expectations of teachers' "duties." Teachers are required to "comply with the Constitution, laws and ethics; serve as role models; implement the national education policy; comply with rules and regulations; implement the school's teaching programs; and fulfill teaching contracts." Teachers are required to teach the students the basic principles of the Constitution and lead students to engage in beneficial social activities. The law specifies the relationship between teacher and student is one in which teachers "care for all students, show respect for their dignity and promote overall development of students in terms of their moral, intellectual and physical development, protect the legitimate rights and interests of the students."

Teacher qualifications are described in several ways in the Teachers Law. Generally, to be eligible to obtain a teaching certificate, teachers are expected to be "Chinese citizens who abide by the Constitution and laws, love education, and have good moral character."

The law makes recommendations for the preparation of teachers, with different levels of preparation depending on the grade level they will be teaching. Kindergarten and primary teachers should be Normal School graduates or above, which means they have completed a senior secondary program in teaching, the equivalent of a high school diploma. Junior secondary teachers and vocational teachers should be normal college or other college graduates or above. Normal colleges are typically two-year programs that specialize in preparing teachers. Senior secondary teachers or technical vocational teachers should be graduates from higher normal college or other university graduate and above. These institutions are typically four-year colleges that culminate in a bachelors' degree. The Teachers Law also extends to teachers in higher education and adult education and sets degree requirements for them as well.

When the Teachers Law was enacted in 1993, it also contained provisions to allow for non-Normal School graduates to gain a teaching certificate. Those who did not have the recommended preparation could apply for a certificate by passing the national qualification examinations as prescribed by the State Council and administered at the provincial level. The provision was partially attempting to address the overall shortage of the teachers being prepared through the Normal School preparation programs as well as attempting to attract students from top tier universities into teaching. Those who had the recommended preparation were exempted from the national qualification examination; they were awarded a teaching certificate when they completed their preparation. College graduates without preparation would have to pass the qualification exam to be awarded a license. Teachers who were already teaching prior to this law going into effect were allowed a transitional time for local authorities to decide on their qualifications. The law also called for the government at various levels "to adopt measures for ethnic minority areas and remote and poor areas to cultivate and train teachers."

Teachers' salaries and benefits are designated within the Teachers' Law to "not be lower or higher than the national average wage of civil servants, and gradually increase." Similarly, teachers are to receive similar medical benefits as civil servant workers and teachers can participate in both national and provincial pension and retirement programs. Schools are expected to establish promotion and pay systems for teachers based on objective measures. Although subsidies for housing in urban and rural areas are identified as a benefit for teachers in the law, it is unclear how widespread this practice is.

The law requires schools to commend and reward teachers who demonstrate outstanding achievement in training, research, education reform, school construction, social services and community organizations or individuals can establish rewards for teachers under strict guidelines by the central government. In 1994, the Teaching Achievement Regulations (Link 5-2) were adopted by the State Council. These regulations defined national awards for collective and individual teaching achievement. The purpose for establishing these awards was described as a way to encourage educators to engage in teaching research and to improve the quality of teaching. The teaching awards are available at the school level, to academic groups, and to individual teachers. Examples of awards that were created under these national regulations include the National Model Teacher Award, the National Education System Award, the Outstanding Teacher Award, and the National Outstanding Educators Award. The awards are recognized in the winner's evaluation records and can be used in applications for rank promotion.

The Chinese Teacher Development Foundation, a partner organization with the MOE, has raised funds through donations and managed the Teacher Incentive Fund since 1986. Since 1998, this fund has been used to enact the awards provision in the Teachers' Law. The Teachers' Incentive Fund has provided nearly 50,000 awards for outstanding teachers and educators. This Incentive Fund has also organized professional activities for about 2 million people. Awards have focused on improving the status of teachers, expanding teachers' influence, educational research, incentives to work in rural and poor areas, and strengthening rural education in China.

Ensuring Ongoing Quality of Teachers: 2004 Continuing Education Requirements

 In 2004 the *Primary and Secondary School Teachers' Continuing Education Requirements* (Link 5-3) were adopted nationally. Continuing education was defined as both a right and an obligation of teachers. All levels of government—national, provincial, county, and township—were charged with ensuring the implementation of the requirements in these regulations. Under these regulations, teachers are required to accumulate at least 240 hours of professional development every five years. Probationary teachers (in their first year of hire) are required to have a minimum of 120 hours of training during that first year.

The regulations require that the substance of teacher training include "ideological and political education and ethics training; updating and expanding the teachers' expertise; modern educational theory and practice; educational research; teaching skills and modern educational technology; modern science and humanities community scientific knowledge." Throughout their continuing education, teachers are expected to continually pursue higher levels of learning for their advancement.

Current Focus on Quality and Distribution of Teaching Expertise: Teachers in the 2020 Plan

The clear focus of the 2020 Plan is on how students experience the education system in China and how they will give back to the nation after they complete their formal education by participating in the workforce and the economy. Generally, the 2020 Plan supports the fundamental idea that schools should be run by experienced educators and they should be supported and acknowledged for their contributions to new ideas and practices. Teachers, within the 2020 Plan, are not specifically discussed in detail until the last section of the reform plan, which is a list of "Guaranteeing Measures" unlike other sections which are focused on systems, strategies, and goals. In this final section, "Strengthening and building of the teachers' contingent" (pp. 36–38) describes the reform focus for teachers and teaching in five categories that have a mixture of reiterating current laws and practices, tightening regulations and administrative procedures, and introducing new approaches to distributing quality teaching across the nation.

First, the reform plan focuses on the quality of teachers by "improving their status, safeguard their rights and interests, raising their salaries and benefits, and turning teaching into a respected occupation" (p. 36). This is a reiteration of existing law and a call for more equitable treatment of teachers in the rural areas who have suffered from low salaries, underpaid salaries, and fewer opportunities for ongoing professional opportunities.

Second, the 2020 Plan calls for promoting the professional ethics among teachers by adopting "a complete package of steps . . . and mechanisms with long-term effects, to foster academic work ethics and atmosphere, overcome impetuosity in scholarship, and investigate and punish any academic misconduct" (p. 37). This call for reform is meant to strengthen the integrity of teaching as some succumb to pressures of performance and to the nonregulated practices of charging fees for preferential treatment of students.

Third, the plan calls for "raising teachers' professional efficiency" (p. 37) by bringing strong focus to the preparation and training of teachers, principals, and vocational instructors. Specifically, the plan calls for the reform of teacher preparation "to construct an open and flexible educational system in which normal universities play the most important role, and comprehensive universities can get involved. The mode of education shall be renovated, fieldwork and other practical activities intensified, training in teachers' work ethics and instruction proficiency stepped up, and the overall training quality promoted" (p. 37). This call for reform responds to criticisms that teacher preparation programming is highly theoretical with less attention to practical activities within classrooms. It also focuses more specifically on the quality of preparation that teachers in the rural areas experience and the minimal training required for vocational teachers at a time when there is a call for increasing vocational educational opportunities for students.

Fourth, teachers' social status, salaries, and benefits are explicitly described in the call for reform by calling for better working, learning, and living conditions for teachers along with performance-based salaries for teachers. The reform plan also calls for special attention to teachers in rural areas to receive increased stipends, better housing arrangements, and teaching awards for distinguished contributions in rural areas. Performance pay for teachers is a relatively new idea in China while the disparities of working conditions in rural areas compared to urban areas is identified several times throughout the call for reform.

Finally, the 2020 Plan sets expectations for "streamlining administration over teachers" (p. 38) through better administration of the teacher credentialing system, clarifying the employment and incentive systems for teachers in schools, and improving the mechanisms for the removal of teachers. This part of the plan also proposes changing the process of rotating compulsory education school teachers and principals to rural areas by requiring urban primary and middle school teachers to "work at least one year in rural schools or schools with disadvantaged teaching facilities and faculty before they can apply for senior titles and positions" (p. 38). With this proposal, the central government is aiming to scale up pilot programs of teacher rotations and make it a requirement for the most experienced teachers to "take a turn" teaching in the lesser resourced areas of the country. For example, Tongling City in Anhui province has been experimenting with this program and working out the details of how many years of rotation to require and support for teachers to rotate from the urban to more regions of the Anhui Province (OECD, 2015).

Responding to the 2020 Plan: 2011 Teaching Standards in China

In response to the 2020 Plan's call for improving the ethics and effectiveness of teaching, the MOE released two sets of professional teaching standards, one for primary teachers and one for secondary teachers in 2011. These standards were developed to align with the Teachers Law and the Compulsory Education Law and to give stronger guidance to teacher preparation programs about the professional expectations for teachers. These standards are organized into four broad categories and then further specified into 61 basic requirements or teaching standards.

The first broad area focuses on establishing a student-centered approach to teaching. These standards speak to respecting the rights and individual personalities of the students; understanding physical and developmental needs of the students; to care for and protect the students. Creating active learning approaches that support independent development, stimulating curiosity, fostering learning interests, and creating freedom to explore are also described as a professional expectation.

The second broad area focuses on the teacher's ethics. China issued a code of ethics for primary and middle school teachers in 2008, asking teachers to "take care of their students' safety." In these new standards, ethics is described in multiple ways and with more emphasis on the teachers' own "professional identity and uniqueness." The standards include expectations of the teacher to serve as a role model and to have a love of the work they do with career aspirations and strong professionalism. Characteristics and behaviors of teachers are spelled out as caring, responsible, patient, careful, optimistic, enthusiastic, cheerful, nice, knowing how to use comic relief, maintaining a peace of mind, eager to learn, neatly dressed, polite manners, and appropriate use of language. Teachers are also expected to live and practice within the socialist core value system.

The third broad area focuses on the theoretical and practical aspects of teaching and has the most standards associated with it. These knowledge and skills standards include general pedagogical knowledge such as classroom management, understanding students' thinking, understanding cultural characteristics and behaviors of students, and understanding overall life development and values formation. They also include disciplinary knowledge and pedagogical content knowledge such as methods and strategies for teaching specific content subjects. General education knowledge is required, including understanding the Chinese educational system, and knowledge of other subjects including art appreciation. Instructional design and teaching implementation standards include lesson plan design based on learning objectives as well those based on personalized learning plans for students. As a signal toward the desire to reform the instructional approaches to foster more innovation and creative thinking within its citizenry, these standards specifically emphasize creating learning environments that "inspire and protect the high school students' interest in learning" and promote instructional approaches such as "heuristic, inquiry, discussion, participatory approaches." The idea of supporting students to "think independently and lead the initiative to explore, develop students' ability to innovate" is specified in these teaching standards. In addition, teachers are expected to be able to integrate technology in instruction, use multiple assessment and evaluation practices, help students to self-evaluate their own performance, communicate effectively with parents, and properly respond to emergencies.

The final broad area of the teaching standards focuses on the teachers' lifelong learning while also contributing to the ongoing development of the whole educational enterprise. These standards specify that teachers should work with their colleagues to share experiences and resources.

Teachers should also take initiative to "collect and analyze relevant information, and constantly reflect and improve education and teaching." To do this, teachers should identify practice need and problems and address them through exploration and research.

How School Structure Shapes Teachers' Work

Many elements of school structure shape the daily work of teachers— how classrooms are organized, how the curriculum is organized, how the school schedule is set up, and the emphasis placed on examinations all contribute to the working lives of teachers. This section will discuss these school structures and how those structures give shape to a teachers' working day and job responsibilities.

The "Class" Grouping of Students

Many of China's approaches to organizing teachers and students in schools were adopted from the Soviet Union in the early 1950s and the long history of Chinese *Shuyuan*, a famous Chinese education institution which focused on the learning of the group and student-teacher relationships. Students in Chinese schools are organized into class groups that stay together across their years within a school. Students may move out of their class if their academic performance (based on test scores) allows them to move to a more advanced class. Nationally, the average student-to-teacher ratio in China was 17:1 in 2013 for elementary schools and 15:1 for secondary schools (MOE, 2015).

OECD (2010) reports that the average student-to-teacher ratio in Shanghai is 14:1. Classes I observed in Shanghai schools had between 22 and 35 students. In schools with high demand, it is not unusual for teachers to have classes of 35–45 students in the elementary grades and 55 to 65 students in junior secondary and secondary grades.

Within this class cohort model, Chinese schools create specialized roles for some teachers and for students. In China, it is typical for each class group to be assigned a teacher called a *banzhuren*—translated as "class director"—who serves as an advisor for the class. This teacher consults with the families of the students, keeps track of the academic progress of the students in the class, and provides counseling to students on social and emotional issues they are facing. Some *banzhurens* are expected to visit the homes and families during the academic year on Saturdays or Sundays or on holidays. The *banzhuren* provides instruction for the class on issues of social importance or will help the class organize themselves into club activities. The *banzhuren* will also sit in on other subjects so she can monitor the progress of her students with other teachers and support them. This cohort or class model for organizing students in schools is argued to provide a stable and predictable learning community for the students and the *banzhuren* gets to know the students and their families by staying with them from grade to grade. The cohort group model is also used at the university level for completing required university courses.

Banzhuren are selected from among the general teaching population of the school and typically have had a few years of teaching experience before taking on the responsibilities of being a *banzhuren*. Typically, a *banzhuren* will continue to teach the subject classes they usually teach in addition to their *banzhuren* duties, with some reduction in their regular teaching load. The *banzhuren* receives additional monthly salary for their role as a *banzhuren* and bonus salary if their class performs well on school placement exams or academic competitions. Traditionally, there has not been any special certification or qualifications for being a *banzhuren*, although that is beginning to change. In 2011, the Shanghai Education Commission set out new training requirements (Link 5-4) for teachers in the *banzhuren* role. These requirements specify 32 hours of training for new *banzhuren* with emphasis on role clarity and the basics principles of the job, 40 hours of training for experienced *banzhuren* with emphasis on community building in schools and with families and adolescent development, and 42 hours of training for lead teachers who have served as *banzhuren* for at least five years with emphasis on classical moral education theories, professionalization of *banzhuren,* and concepts of democracy in classroom management in support of citizenship education.

Specialized student roles within the class include serving as the *zhirisheng*, or the student-on-duty, in their class by sweeping the classrooms, cleaning hallways, serving meals, being class monitors, and helping teachers. Each class is also organized into a class association, with an elected chairman, vice chairman, and conveners of different tasks or clubs. Additionally, student monitors, who wear special armbands to identify their status, monitor hallway behavior, watch to make certain students are doing their twice-daily eye exercises properly, and provide leadership on the marching field during morning exercises. Students complete these tasks very seriously and with pride.

Organizing the Physical Space of the School

This class grouping structure impacts how the physical environment of the school is organized. Students are assigned a desk in their classroom and typically keeping their personal belongings there. The class is tasked with decorating the classroom to personalize it and make it feel like their space. The degree to which this decoration can happen can depend dramatically on the local economic resources of the school community. Some classrooms have plants, curtains, tables with cloth covers, and small in-class libraries. Other classrooms are decorated with only chalk drawings on the blackboard.

For their core required subjects, students stay in their classroom at their desk and the teachers come to them to teach a lesson. Teachers will stay with a class group of students for several years. With students "belonging to" a classroom each year and teachers traveling to those classrooms to conduct lessons, teachers do not locate themselves in a single classroom. The teachers' professional space is in an office that is shared with several other teachers in the school (Figure 5.1). Each teacher typically has a desk and file space in these large working rooms. Teachers use their desk and this office space to prepare for class, grade papers, and meet with students for one-on-one tutoring sessions. At any given time of day there are a handful of teachers in the office during their nonteaching class periods. Meetings among groups of teachers are typically held in conference rooms within the school.

During my school visits, visiting the shared office space of teachers within the schools was like walking into a beehive of activity. On one occasion, one teacher stood in the back of the room talking with two students who were there to get some additional explanation about their homework assignment, three teachers were conferring with each other over schedules and lessons, and two teachers sat at their desks marking papers. The teachers' office gave a strong presence of the professional work in which teachers engage that is work other than being in front of the class of students. Designing lessons, giving feedback on written work, and consulting with students was all a visible part of the daily work of teaching within this shared professional space.

Teachers as Curriculum Specialists

School curriculum determines the areas in which teachers are certified to teach and organizes the teachers into subject area specializations. Each teacher is specialized in a subject matter area, even at the elementary school level. Four major subjects are taught in Chinese schools: Chinese language and culture (these classes include moral and character education and are often rooted in Chinese history and cultural traditions [Link 5-5]), mathematics, science (inclusive of physics, chemistry, and

Figure 5.1 Map of Qilun Primary School, Minhang
District, Shanghai showing the school structure
centered on grade level classes and teachers' offices.

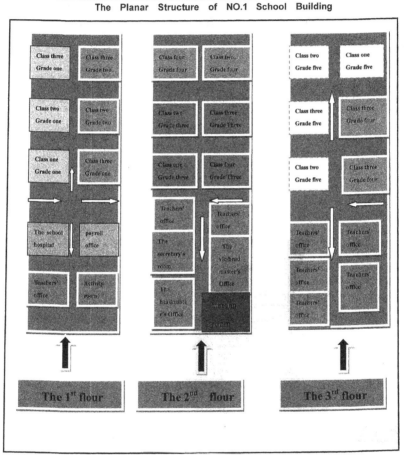

biology), and social science (geography, history, ideology and political science). In primary school, students also have music, fine arts, physical education, and technology. In senior secondary school students typically have fewer electives. Some schools may also offer vocational subjects or specialize in vocational areas.

Curriculum in China is standardized nationwide with provinces having some local control over selection of teaching materials with central government approval. Given the vast nature of the educational system and the regional differences, multiple sets of textbooks at various levels are approved by the MOE to meet the local needs within different regions.

> In 1986, the MOE adopted a policy of diversifying the preparation and production of school textbooks in the whole country under the condition that unified basic requirements must be complied with. In areas where conditions permit, regional educational departments, educational institutions, experts, scholars and individual teachers are encouraged to compile textbooks for subjects taught in primary and junior secondary schools in compliance with the basic requirements set forth in the syllabuses of 9-year compulsory education schooling.
>
> (China Education Center, n.d.)

To ensure the quality of text and teaching materials in terms of "ideological content, scientific spirit and adaptability to classroom instruction" (China Education Center, n.d.), all textbooks for required subjects are examined and approved within the MOE. Other teaching materials such as reference manuals for teachers, wall charts, audiovisual materials, are also produced to complement and supplement textbooks. Some supplementary teaching materials are designed to have local references and traditions to support local economic and cultural development. These supplementary teaching materials are approved by provincial-level authorities.

Textbooks and workbooks are provided for the students free of charge. Students regularly mark up their textbooks with highlighters and annotations. Textbooks are regularly updated and often have moral lessons about hard work, integrity, and protecting the environment built into the information and exercises. For example, during one of my school visits, I observed an English lesson in a primary school. During the lesson, the students read a short description about pandas in English and answered a few questions about pandas and their habitat in English. The teacher led the students through some choral pronunciations of new words. The underlying content of the lesson, though, was strongly centered on understanding the panda as a treasure of the nation of China and a moral lesson in what people can do to protect the pandas' habitat and be good stewards of this national treasure.

The School Schedule

The school schedule determines the working hours for teachers' work as well as how their time is structured during the school day. School typically begins around 8:00 a.m. and ends around 4:00 p.m. Students typically have four to five 40- to 50-minute lessons in the morning, and three to four lessons in the afternoon with at least a 10-minute break between each lesson (at elementary level, lessons are a standard 35 minutes). Many schools expect mandatory study halls in the late afternoon or evening with monitored attendance. Students report usually staying up late into the night to complete homework (see Figure 5.2).

In a given week, a primary teacher will teach 15 hours per week and secondary teachers will teacher about 12 hours per week. The remaining time during the school day is used to take care of other responsibilities associated with teaching: grading papers, preparing lessons for classes, meeting with other teachers to design lessons, conducting classroom and school-based research, and meeting with students. For teachers in China, their time is spent primarily in instructional interactions with students, in collaboration with peers, or in preparing their own lessons and marking papers. It is not typical for teachers to have supervisory responsibilities for children during lunch time, hall passing time, or during breaks in the school day. For example, between classes (which lasts anywhere between

Figure 5.2 A typical school schedule for a senior secondary student.

	Monday	Tuesday	Wednesday	Thursday	Friday
8:00 - 8:40	Class Meeting	Chinese	Physics	Math	Math
8:50 - 9:30	Chinese	Biology	English	Chinese	P.E.
9:30 - 9:50	Morning Exercises				
9:50 - 10:30	Math	Math	Chemistry	History	Biology
10:40 - 11:20	English	Chemistry	Chinese	English	History
11:20 - 11:30	Eye Muscle Relaxation Exercises				
11:30 - 12:10	History/Geography	English	Biology	Politics	Chemistry
12:10 - 2:00	Lunch Break				
2:00 - 2:40	Math	Elective	Math	Physics	English
2:50 - 3:30	Politics	Elective	P.E.	Biology	Chinese
3:40 - 4:20	Physics	Self-Study	Youth League Activity		Quiz
4:30 - 6:00	Extracurricular Activity (e.g., music, sport)				
6:00 - 7:00	Dinner				
7:00 - 12:00	Homework				

10 to 20 minutes) and at lunch time teachers provide very minimal supervision of students except for the teachers designated as *banzhuren*. In Shanghai, the *banzhuren* stay with the students for lunch and use this time to nurture and support peer relationships and social development of the students.

Examinations

Finally, the emphasis on examinations in Chinese secondary schools shapes the daily work of many teachers. Chinese education is sometimes described as being a merit-based system which suggests that the individual's work ethic and effort put into preparing oneself is what determines one's success. This is reflected in the strong tradition of basing advancement and promotion on examination scores. Advancement to both senior secondary school and placement within the higher education system is determined primarily on examination results. The *gaokao*—literally translates to higher examination—is offered once a year in June and students take it at the end of their last year of senior secondary school. Required exams are taken in Chinese, mathematics, and foreign language, and students choose to take either the social sciences or sciences exams. If students do not score well enough to place into one of the colleges or universities of their choice, many will wait another year to retake the exam in hopes of placing into their choice schools the second time. The seriousness of the exam culture in China cannot be overstated. Understanding the support and stress that families experience over these high-stakes exams is deeply rooted in history, hope, and incalculable investment in a child's education. The following excerpt from a blog by an American who teaches in China gives an outsiders' perspective on how families treat the *gaokao*.

> These national exams (the *gaokao*) were given on June 7 and 8. Local middle schools were used as test sites and those middle school students had a two day holiday. The test is of such great significance that parents rent hotel rooms nearby so their student can have a quiet lunch and take a nap. I saw one hotel with a big banner wishing students luck on the exam. Students will take either the liberal arts test or the science test. For liberal arts students, the first test, Chinese, was from 9:00–11:30. Students were dismissed and came back for the math test from 3:00–5:00. On Friday, the schedule was the same, with the morning session being geography, politics, and history and the afternoon session being English. The parents filled the street in front of the school and anxiously awaited students coming

from the test sites and wanted to know how their child did. Taxi cabs even offer free service to these students to help them get home or to the testing site. My friend Kevin's uncle took time off work to drive Kevin to the test site, pick him up at noon to take him home, then bring him back. It is huge deal!

(Dalian Diary Blog, 2007)

For junior secondary and senior secondary teachers, the *gaokao* exam and other academic competitions shape their work in two ways. First, teachers feel a great responsibility to prepare their students for the high-stakes exams and other competitions. Teachers feel that it is their responsibility to ensure the success of their students on the *gaokao* since the results of this test determine the type of higher education that the students can pursue. For senior secondary teachers, this typically results in teaching practices that are tightly linked to exam preparation and narrows the educational experiences between the teachers and the students. Professor Cheng Pingyuan, a professor of Nanjing Normal University, reported in a national study of the examination pressure that, "The pursuit of high test scores not only brings pressure to students, but also to teachers, making the relationship between teachers and students worse, especially when students perform poorly in exams . . ." (Zhao, 2014). Second, teachers are rewarded for the performance of their students on high-stakes examinations through performance pay and in their reputation as a teacher who has prepared student to be successful.

Policy makers, many educators, and some families believe that *zhongkao* and *gaokao* examinations is placing undue stress on students and prohibiting the development of other talents and ways of thinking. In worse case scenarios, the pressures of the exams have led to adolescent suicides (Zhao, 2014). Calls for curriculum and instructional reform are present in policy documents, academic arguments, and from some corners of the community. Critiques of the current stress-ridden educational approach are articulated at all levels of the educational system, yet families and traditions of the merit-based ideals of individual advancement through ones' earned performance on examinations continue to ground China's education system.

Teaching Practices in China

People in the West tend to hold a view of China's schools as an exam-driven system with crowded classrooms. These characterizations are true to some extent as I have already reported. However, the Chinese educational system is also imbued with a sense of building strong community within the classroom, establishing and supporting strong relationships between schools and families, and an increasing effort to make class-room instruction more dynamic and participatory for students as I have reported in describing the class cohort model, the role of the *banzhuren*, and the increasing critiques of the reliance on examinations. This section and the following section describe the general instructional approaches used in Chinese and Shanghai classrooms, challenging the assumption that teaching and learning is based on lecture and memorization.

Teaching practices in China are more diverse than the stereotype of all lecture and all rote memorization, as illustrated in Figure 5.3. While just over two-thirds of teachers in this survey report using lecture at least some of the time, they also use a wide range of other methods, ranging from col-laborative learning and discussion to role play, simulations, and storytelling. Note that teachers could choose more than one type of teaching method on the survey, resulting in more than 100 total percentage points reported.

Teaching practices also vary according to the schooling level. Teach-ers in the primary schools are working to instill more and more learning activities in their classroom instruction in response to national curriculum reforms and calls for students to develop creative problem-solving skills. As students approach levels of schooling with examination gateways—at the end of junior secondary school and the end of senior secondary school—the pressures to prepare the students for their exam performance increases. The students' results on the examinations will determine the quality of schooling they will be allowed to pursue. These high-stakes examinations create pressure for both families and teachers to do what they think will best support the students in performing well. For second-

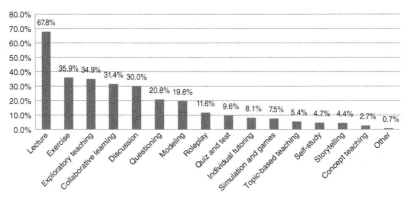

Figure 5.3 Application of teaching methods

Gang, 2010, p. 104, Figure 4–6.

ary teachers, this often results in teaching strategies that are more lecture and direct instruction oriented.

Teaching and Learning in Shanghai

Most analysts agree that when watching teachers with students in Shanghai, there is an expectation and a demand that every student can succeed. And there is a general understanding that students and families in Shanghai are invested in the importance of education. Some observers of classrooms in Shanghai from OECD report, "There's real interest and engagement between teachers and students . . . Every Shanghai classroom has high demands yet offers extensive support" (Jiang, 2011).

A 2005 survey of Shanghai students and parents conducted by the Shanghai Education Information Investigation Team showed that 90.46% of students and 86.59% of parents agree that their teachers are very keen to help the students when they face learning difficulties (Tan, 2013, pp. 34–35). During my observations and interviews, teachers talked about how to motivate students during the lesson, how to engage students in participatory ways during the lesson, and how to extend the lesson to help students learn for themselves. I observed mathematics lessons based on complex problems, art lessons that expected individuality and creativity, science lessons in which students engaged with real-world phenomena, and Chinese lessons that addressed current social and environmental issues that need solutions.

For example, during one school site visit, I observed a fifth-grade mathematics lesson in Qilun Elementary School in Minhang District, a district that is not in the wealthiest city center and has several manufacturing facilities as the economic base (Link 5-6). The lesson was a demonstration lesson, meaning that a formal lesson plan had been prepared for several observers to see in advance and for observing teachers to be able to discuss after the lesson was completed. The lesson plan is shown in Figure 5.4 and was considered to be a typical design for a lesson plan in this school.

The lesson plan is a very important part of teaching in Shanghai. Lesson design is a tightly choreographed activity that usually involves the input from many teachers within the school. For lessons that will be used as demonstration lessons for other schools or in competitions, the lesson will be taught and modified based on feedback from several teachers. In many schools the lesson plans have to be approved by the subject area lead teacher, or, in smaller schools, by the principal.

In this lesson plan, we can see that the teacher begins with an analysis of the textbook and explores the mathematical concepts that she is

Figure 5.4   Lesson plan for fifth-grade mathematics lesson given at Qilun Elementary School in Minhang District, Shanghai in November 2013.

School: Qilun Elementary School in Minhang District	Class: 5th grade, class 2	Instructor: Jiaying Zhang
Topic: Learning about features of parallelogram	No. of students: 22	Date: November 19, 2013

1. Teaching objectives

1) To transfer methods of studying rectangle and square, and lead students to self-discover features of parallelogram from the dimensions of "side" and "angle".

2) To experience the instability of parallelogram in creative activities, and discover relationships between parallelogram, rectangle, and square.

2. Rationales for the objectives

1) Textbook analysis

Parallelogram appears in lesson 5, volume 10, of the elementary math textbook. In the textbook, parallelogram is introduced through two transparent color bands in parallel intersecting, then acknowledging two opposite sides to be of equal length and opposite angles to be of equal degrees, followed by an exploration of its diagonal, base, and height. I think this process takes separate approaches to understanding its sides and angles, and it lacks a comparison and connection with rectangle and square that have been introduced. As a matter of fact, learning of shape features falls into two stages: the first one is an understanding of features based on an understanding of elements, learning about superordinate concept, superordinate method and structure, and learning about features of rectangle and square through numbers of sides and angels, and the degrees of the angles. The second stage is based on an understanding of connections, when learning is about the numbers and degrees as well as about the locations of sides and degrees. This lesson falls into the second stage.

In learning about features of two-dimensional shapes that have similar structure, it works to test hypotheses and draw conclusions, continuously exploring its features, and being creative in using the features. The learning of parallelogram is based on learning about features of rectangle, square, and triangle. From the latter students have acquired knowledge, methods, and process and could transfer these to the learning of parallelogram. Then, they can be supported to make further comparison with features of rectangle, square, and triangle, to discuss their connections, and to enhance their understanding of these shapes. It is important to help students learn in a process of understanding features from different perspectives, thus to solidify their knowledge structure of shapes.

2) Student learning analysis

Before this lesson, students have observed parallelogram. Although they are not yet able to articulate its features, they can tell which shape is a parallelogram. In the first stage of learning, they have explored features of rectangle, square, and triangle, and learned to explore features of shapes from the two dimensions of "side" and "angle", and acquired the basic process of exploring features of shapes: making hypotheses — test hypotheses — summary and conclusion — making connections. The prior knowledge that students have lays a foundation for an active discovery of the topic in this lesson.

There are challenges in the discovery indeed. First, they might not know how to describe the angles in parallelogram because the concept of opposite angles has not been introduced yet; second, due to possible measure errors, the best way to prove opposite sides to be of equal length is to see if they coincide. Yet parallelogram is not of axial symmetry, it is hard to prove the opposite sides coincide; third, rectangle is a parallelogram with four right angles. It involves a complex process to learn the concept that rectangle is a special parallelogram; fourth, a rectangle is a parallelogram with four right angles. If four sides were equal in a rectangle, it becomes a square. The path from a parallelogram to a square involves changes in side and then in angle. How to make students think further about the connections in addition to an understanding? These challenges need a breakthrough from previous research methods.

Teaching procedures			
Stages	Teacher activities	Students' activities	Purpose
1. Regular accumulation	Display: square, rectangle Summary: We can explore features of two-dimensional shapes from the dimensions of "side" and "angle".	Talk about features and connections to your desk neighbors.	Review prior learning and get ready for the learning that comes up next.
2. Exploring features of parallelogram	Step 1. Making hypotheses Question: The instructor gives each student a parallelogram. You all know that parallelogram is a shape with four sides and four angles. Please mark the four angles with <1, <2, <3, <4. Take a close look at the four sides and angles, and see what features they have.	Think, write, and talk with your desk neighbor. Share and make hypothesis. Test hypothesis.	Based on students' prior experiences of studying rectangular, square, and triangular, lead them to actively apply the same knowledge structure in the process of "making hypothesis — test hypothesis — draw conclusion", to experience and learn about the features of parallelogram.

	Ask students to share their thoughts: 1) side: opposite sides in parallel and of equal length 2) angle: <1=<3, <2=<4 Step 2. Exploring features Question: Do all parallelogram share the features? You will see many types of parallelogram in the bag. Please test if your hypothesis is correct. Group sharing: 1) features of side: Hint: Could you use a tool to see if the opposite sides coincide? 2) features of angle: Introduction: the concept of opposite angles Step 3. Drawing conclusions Question: Through hypothesis testing, what conclusions can you draw about features of side and angle in a parallelogram? Definition: Parallelogram is a shape with four sides, of which opposite sides that are in parallel.	Explore: Given the possibility of measure errors, it works to see if opposite sides coincide. It is hard to prove that opposite sides in parallelogram coincide. You can do so by rotating it. Clarification: In a parallelogram, opposite sides are in parallel and of equal length. Opposite angles are of equal degrees.	The process will focus on the challenges students might have. For example, let students experience if opposite sides can coincide.

3. Exploring instability of parallelogram	Task: With short sticks, how will you create a parallelogram? Why? Make a parallelogram using the short sticks.	Clarification: Because parallelogram has two opposite sides of equal length, you may select two short sticks of equal length.	In the discovery, students will go through scientific and logic process. In twisting parallelogram, they will see changes in the angles, and learn that rectangular is a special type of parallelogram. In comparing parallelogram with triangle, they will further understand the instability of parallelogram.
	Question: With the same sticks, the parallelograms you've created are different. Compare the sides and angles of your parallelograms; are there anything similar and different?	Compare thoughts: Sides being the same, angles have changed. Thoughts on the experiment. Focus on one particular angle. Mark the degrees of each angle, like 30, 45, 60, 90, 120, 135.	
	Task: Now try making a stable parallelogram using four short sticks. See how many types of parallelograms can you make? Is there any special case?	Share findings: Rectangular is a special type of parallelogram with all features of parallelogram. The unique feature of rectangular is that it has four right angles.	
	Guide: When observing changes in angles, you may focus on one angle and see how the others change accordingly.	Thoughts: It is not easy to twist the triangle. It is much easier to twist the parallelogram. Share the application in life.	
	Comparison: I have a triangle here. Let's twist it. What can you find?		
	Summary and further exploration: Parallelogram is not stable. Can you recall where in our life parallelogram is used because of its instability?		

4. Exploring connections between parallelogram and other shapes	Question: This is a parallelogram. How can we make it a rectangle? How can we make a rectangle a square? Share findings. Follow-up question: Change the angles, and then the sides. Is there any other way to make a parallelogram a square? Summary: Shapes can be transformed according to their features. Task: There seems to be close connections between parallelogram, rectangle, and square. Can you draw a picture to display the connections? Summary: Square is a special type of rectangle. Rectangle is a special type of parallelogram.	Think and share. Thoughts: Change the angles to 90 degrees, and the side to equal length. Share findings: You may change side length first to a diamond shape, and then angles to make a square. Share with your desk neighbor. Try drawing a picture. Exploring the connections: From the outer layer to the center: Parallelogram Rectangle Square	The exploration of connections will further enhance their understanding of the features and help make connections. The picture vividly displays the connections among the three shapes, which also lays a foundation for future learning.
5. Summary of the lesson	Summary: How have we explored the features of parallelogram? We can study other shapes using the same method.	Pair and share.	This is to further build the knowledge structure, and inspire students to actively apply learning in related study.

planning to teach. Her analysis shows her deep knowledge of the mathematics as an elementary teacher. She raises questions about how the textbook represents the geometric concepts and introduces her own thinking about how to build understanding of polygons and their relationship to their component parts.

The lesson plan then shows how the teacher analyzes the learning objectives through the lens of student learning. The teacher is aware of what the students have learned about polygons prior to this lesson, the challenges the students might face in exploring new ideas about angles within polygons, and how she might help them make stronger connections between what they already know and the new concepts she is introducing in the lesson. The approach to teaching in this analysis shows us that the teacher relies on both her knowledge of the mathematical concepts as well as her knowledge of how the students will engage with the ideas. She concludes her analysis with a question— "How to make students think further about the connections in addition to an understanding?" The teacher is not only describing what she knows, but also illustrates the research mindset of a Shanghai teacher. Instruction is a place to ask questions and learn more about how students are learning in order to continually refine teaching practices.

The lesson plan shows the teachers' thinking behind her instruction. In the details of how the lesson will unfold, we see the teaching and learning strategies including teacher questioning, the use of hands-on manipulatives, student hypothesizing, and students sharing their ideas in pairs. There is a lot of activity packed into the 35-minute lesson period, making the pace of the lesson fast paced and nonstop.

During the actual lesson, the teacher stayed true to the lesson plan and the students were engaged from the moment the teacher entered the room until she dismissed them. In the post-lesson debrief, the observers made several suggestions for improving the lesson. One teacher suggested having the students actively work through the process of making a hypothesis about the structure of the parallelogram before exploring with the materials and then drawing conclusions about what they find through their exploration. Another teacher suggested making the materials for the activity more challenging by having different lengths of sticks for building the polygons to allow the students more freedom to explore a wider variety of relationships. A principal commented that the questions the teacher asked of the students should be "bigger" questions that would allow the students to find relationships by themselves rather than the direct teacher question and student response that he observed during the lesson. All of these suggestions are supportive of an approach to teaching that is driven by more student thinking and engagement with the learning process and trying to direct the teachers' role into one that designs materials and activities that support student exploration and draw out their own conclusions.

NOTES

1. All quotes used within the discussion of the national policies related to teaching are taken directly from the English translations of the national laws and regulations which can be found on the Ministry of Education website and the Database of Laws and Regulations of the PRC government. When page numbers are available in the policy documents, they are provided. See the reference section for the URLs of these websites.

6

TEACHER PREPARATION IN CHINA AND SHANGHAI

THE MINISTRY OF EDUCATION (MOE) sets the general curriculum guidelines for all teacher training through the Department of Teacher Education. The MOE is responsible for providing policy and curriculum guidance for the higher education institutions which oversee teacher preparation. The provincial and municipal Education Commissions are responsible for coordinating teacher training with higher education institutions. Since 2001, the Ministry has been shifting the governance of teacher education from centralized control to creating a system that allows more local governance and decision making around curriculum and assessment of candidates in accordance with new standards for teaching rather than through a national curriculum for teacher education.

Teacher Preparation Minimum Expectations

As was described earlier, the Teachers' Law recommends that teachers have a minimum of Normal School training prior to being certified as teachers. Within this system, an elementary teacher should have at minimum a high school diploma, a junior secondary school teacher should have at minimum an associates' degree or the equivalent of two years of postsecondary education, and an upper secondary teachers should have, at minimum, a bachelor's degree based on four years of postsecondary education (Ingersoll, 2007). Teachers can also be prepared through programs that exceed these expectations.

The majority of teachers in China complete formalized teacher preparation programs prior to taking the teaching certification exam. Since 1986, however, comprehensive universities have been encouraged to recruit their graduates to become teachers. This allows students in some of the higher ranked universities to take the teacher certification exam and receive a teaching certification without completing formalized teacher preparation. This loosening of the entry preparation requirements for teaching is in response to the teacher shortages that the country is facing and a policy effort to encourage more high-performing college students from the top tier universities to choose teaching as their career. Based on the teacher self-reports in Figure 6.1, only 4% of elementary teachers, 2.5% of junior secondary teachers, and 3.2% of senior secondary teachers reported having no formal training in teaching prior to beginning their teaching career.

Nationally, the majority of teachers hold a four-year college degree (71.7% in urban, 69.2% county schools), although in townships and rural schools, teachers with only two-year college degrees outnumber teachers with four-year college degrees (39.0% are four-year college graduates and 47.8% are two-year college graduates) (see Figure 6.1). The small percentage of teachers with only middle school education backgrounds are likely teachers nearing retirement who became teachers after the Cultural Revolution and community members took up teaching as the school systems were being rebuilt. Given the disparity of resources

Figure 6.1 Teachers' educational background and academic degrees in various regions

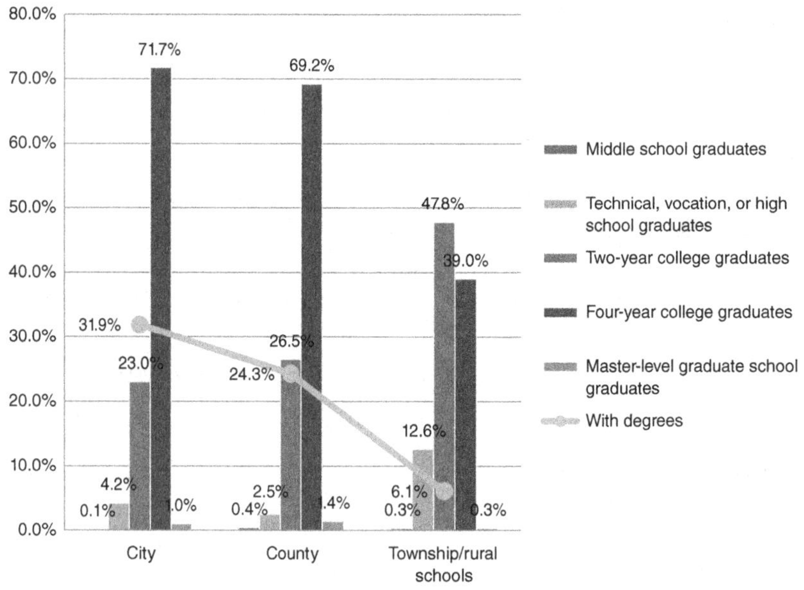

Gang, 2010, p. 12, Figure 4.

across the nation, western China has greater difficulty recruiting and retaining teachers in the poorer, rural towns and villages and these areas compensate by hiring teachers who do not have the full required educational experience for teacher certification.

From a policy perspective, China has been trying to improve its teaching force through certification requirements and incentives to teach in rural and border areas. There are efforts under way to increase the educational qualifications for elementary teachers across China. For example, the number of Normal Schools at the senior secondary level for primary school teaching certification (equivalent to a high school degree for preparing to be an elementary teacher) decreased from 892 in 1997 to 430 in 2002 as the local or provincial teacher education requirements for certification of preschool and elementary school teachers increased (Ministry of Education, 1999, 2005 as cited in Zhu & Han, 2006) and the number of elementary school teachers who hold two-year degrees from normal colleges increased to 40% in 2003 (Ministry of Education, 2003 as cited in Zhu & Han, 2006).

At the same time that the country is aiming to improve the preparation and quality of its teaching force through more preparation requirements, China has also been experimenting with a Teach for China program modeled after the Teach for America program in the United States since 2009. Teach for China recruits academically able college graduates from China and the United States—called "Fellows"—and trains them to serve as full-time teachers for two years in underresourced Chinese schools. According to the Teach for All website (the parent organization for Teach for China), the program has placed 5 cohorts totaling 335 teachers in 98 schools in both rural and urban areas. Rather than participating in Normal School preparation, Fellows undergo an intensive training program including pedagogy and Chinese language skills (for American Fellows). Following this training program, Fellows are placed in underresourced schools in Yunnan and Guangdong provinces. At their schools, Teach For China Fellows are full-time members of the faculty and receive a salary commensurate to that of local teachers in their placement regions. American Fellows typically teach English language, while Chinese Fellows teach other core subjects such as science, math, geography, and ethics.

In 2001, Shanghai instituted its Teacher Qualification System, putting into place the following minimum requirements for entering teaching in Shanghai:

- All teacher candidates should undergo professional training and pass the tests in the following areas of study: pedagogy, educational psychology, and teaching methods.

○ All teachers in kindergartens or primary schools must hold a level of education minimally higher than the preschool teacher training schools or the teacher training schools (at least senior secondary education).

○ Teachers in general junior high schools must possess an educational qualification at least equivalent to or higher than that provided by the teacher training college or other colleges for professional training (at least a Bachelor's degree).

○ Teachers in general senior high schools or vocational secondary schools must hold an educational qualification at least equivalent to or higher than a regular university or other universities (at least a Bachelor's degree).

○ Fieldwork supervisors in vocational secondary schools hold an educational qualification at least equivalent to or higher than vocational secondary schools (at least a Bachelor's degree). (Zhang, Xu, & Sun, 2014, p. 146)

These minimum requirements for entering teaching in Shanghai are slightly higher for junior secondary teachers than is required by the national minimal requirements. In practice, however, the overall educational background of Shanghai's teaching force is considerably higher than in most parts of China. More than 60% of the primary school teachers in Shanghai hold a bachelor's degree and about 6% of the secondary school teachers hold a master's degree. Recent reports suggest that "possessing a Bachelor's degree with some kind of teacher professional training has become the new threshold for all the new entrants to the teaching profession in Shanghai" (Zhang, Xu, & Sun, 2014, p. 146).

Teacher Preparation Program Design

Even with some latitude for local design of programs with approval from the MOE, teacher preparation curriculum is very similar across the country (Liang et al., 2012). Teacher preparation for primary school teachers typically has four parts. First, required courses in educational history, psychology, and sociology are considered a core part of the preparation program. These courses include ideological and political education and Chinese (including methods of Chinese teaching). Second, required courses in a content domain are typically chosen from an area of specialization from among the social sciences, math and natural science, or performing and fine arts. Both primary teachers and secondary teachers specialize in subject matter content within these content domains. Third, optional courses are based on the regional education needs and may include vocational and technical subjects that align with local economic development. Finally, pedagogy and teaching practice courses may include age-appropriate pedagogy courses, audiovisual education, basics of computer applications, handwriting (on paper and on the chalkboard or whiteboard), practicum in schools, and a practice teaching experience.

Teacher preparation programs for secondary teaching place most emphasis on subject area specialization. Programs also include courses on politics, physical culture, pedagogy, and child psychology. Programs typically have teaching practice in schools in the third and fourth years of the program. Figure 6.2 illustrates the kinds of training that teachers have during their preparation based on a national survey of teachers. The activities with the highest occurrence are taking psychology courses, followed by education foundation courses. The lowest occurrences (not counting "other" and "none") are volunteer teaching (a self-initiated activity that is generally not a requirement of teacher preparation programs in Normal Schools) and general pedagogy courses.

Figure 6.2 Teachers' participation in professional training before teaching at all levels of schooling

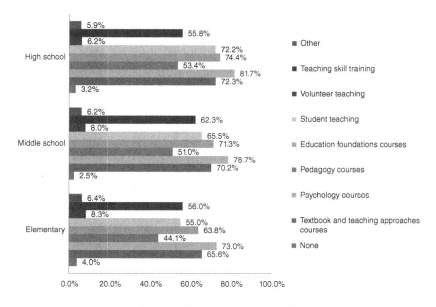

Gang, 2010, p. 49, Figure 2–5.

In Shanghai, teacher preparation has been fully incorporated into the two normal universities in the city—Shanghai Normal University, a provincial-run institution, and East China Normal University, a comprehensive university with national ranking. Not all of Shanghai's teachers are prepared at these universities, but most graduates from Shanghai Normal University will enter teaching in Shanghai since they are typically from Shanghai, while East China Normal University students are drawn from across the country and will gain teaching positions in other provinces also. Incorporating all teacher preparation within the normal universities in Shanghai means that the selection mechanism for universities (via performance on the *gaokao* exam) is now an integral part of entering a teacher preparation program in the city.

Shanghai Normal University prepares primary school teachers in a four-year bachelor's degree program. Students typically take general education courses in their first year, comprising topics such as education theory, pedagogy, educational psychology, moral principles, foreign history of education, educational research methods, sociology of education, philosophy of education, education management, human resources development and management, social psychology, family education, and education evaluation (Shanghai Normal University website). In their second year of the program, students take foundational courses in their major field of study—social sciences, math and natural sciences, or performance or fine arts.

In their third year, students experience a two-week teaching practice placement in each term while continuing to take content and educational courses. Students in the fall 2013 focus group reported what they observe in a school. Figure 6.3 shows how this "First Student Teaching" experience is structured by the university. The students complete five assignments during this practicum period: they observe the physical layout of the school, they interview a school leader to learn about the school mission, they interview a school leader to learn about the school as an organization, they interview a teacher to learn about the students in the school and the teachers' approach to teaching, and they interview the dean of student affairs to learn about the school curriculum. Finally, the students complete an overall reflection on what they have learned from this school-based learning experienced. These assignments engage the students in understanding how schools operate and what the work of teaching looks like from a broad perspective.

In their fourth and last year of their degree, the students spend eight weeks in an internship practice teaching. The university provides options of schools for the candidates to select for their various practice experiences. The schools are typically considered high-performing schools in the city.

Figure 6.3 Teaching practicum assignments for third year college students at Shanghai Normal University.

College of Education
Shanghai Normal University

Elementary Education
(Shi Cheng class)
Practice Report
(1ˢᵗ student teaching)

Grade _____ Name _____ Student ID _____

May 2013

Assignment #1. Observing the school buildings and layout in the placement site

1. Walk around the school, observe the school buildings
Use the following table for observation. Tick the things you see and cross out those you don't see. Add things that you see and are not listed in the table.

For teaching	Regular classrooms	Specialized/assigned classroom	Classroom for public or shared use
		Science classroom Language classroom Calligraphy classroom Dancing classroom Swimming pool History and geography classroom Computer classroom Art classroom Music classroom Indoors playground Labor work classroom	Combined classroom Student activity room Psychology consulting room Office for subject teachers Library Physiology test room Moral education exhibition room
For administration	Administration offices such as the principal's, 教务 Student organization or club office Printing room Main office Internet monitor room Mail room Archive room Conference room News and broadcasting room Public securities monitor room Clinic Warehouse and maintenance room		
For service	Drinking water Kitchen Facilities room Shower room Bathroom Food delivery room Canteen Garage		

2. Draw a floor plan of the school and paste photos of some school buildings you take. School floor plan:

Photos of school buildings:

Assignment #2. Interview an elementary school leader. Ask him to introduce the school mission and education goals.

Interview time: _____ Interviewee: _____

Basic information of the school	School name			
	School address		Phone	
	No. of teachers		No. of students	
Interview content	School mission			
	Education goals			
	School motto			
Analysis	Analyze the relation between school mission and education goals, and how the connection is represented.			

Assignment #3. Interview an elementary school leader. Ask him to introduce the school organization and connections of each department. Draw a diagram to show the school organization.

Interview time: _____ Interviewee: _____

School			
Address		Phone	
Interview content	Name of departments in the school organization		
	Connections of each department		
Analysis	Draw a diagram to show the school organization. Analyze the interview data.		

Assignment #4. Interview a teacher to know characteristics of elementary students' physiological and psychological development, and pedagogical strategies that teachers use accordingly.

		Evidence	Pedagogical strategies
Characteristics of physiological development			
Characteristics of psychological development			

Assignment #5. Interview the Dean of student affairs. Ask him to introduce the school curriculum plan to understand the school curriculum and curriculum structure. Draw a diagram to show the curriculum.

Interview time: _____ Interviewee: _____

School			
Address		Phone	
Interview content	Curriculum		
	Curriculum structure		
Analysis	Draw a diagram to show the curriculum. Analyze the interview data.		

Classroom Teaching Observation notes			
No#:	Course title:	Learning theme:	
Class:	No. of students:	Instructor:	Location:
Date:	Observer:	Note:	
Classroom teaching process (real-time):			Formative comments:
Analysis of classroom teaching activities			

Summary of student teaching I

Placement site			Placement dates		
Basic information	Classroom observation	( ) periods	Including	Classes in the major	( ) periods
				Classes not in the major	( ) periods
				Research (exploratory) class	( ) periods
Personal summary					

The university also invites accomplished teachers of high rank to give lectures for the university students. During practice teaching the teacher candidates have a guiding teacher or mentor in the school and a mentor from the university who is typically a professor. The candidates learn how to develop lesson plans, how to deliver a lesson, how to work with children, how to run a class (remembering that the students are kept as a class cohort through their school experience), how to communicate with parents, how to use particular pedagogies such as story time or mathematics manipulatives, and how to recognize the areas that they need to work on in their teaching skills.

Students in the focus group reported that they thought that the practice component of their preparation program was the most important part of their program. They report feeling like they learned more about teaching by engaging with practicing teachers in the schools and that they sometimes have difficulty making connections between what they have learned in their course work to the real work of teaching they experience during their internship. This criticism of teacher preparation program design has also made its way into policy discussions with some emphasis in the 2020 Plan on improving the relationship between theory and practice in teacher preparation. Students value the practical experiences they have and seek out their own practical teaching experience by volunteering in schools within their own community. Each focus group participant had taken on some volunteer teaching role, paid tutoring work, or teaching English in programs for business people in order to gain more practical experience. It seemed that the volunteer practical experience was a de facto part of the curriculum for teacher preparation.

Secondary school teachers are prepared at both East China Normal University and Shanghai Normal University. The curriculum is similar in that it requires both courses in education and content specialization courses and an eight-week student teaching internship. Whereas primary teacher preparation is the responsibility of education faculty, secondary teacher preparation in the content areas resides in the various academic departments of the universities and only the pedagogical and education courses are taught by the education faculty.

Students at the Meng Xianchen College at East China Normal University are experiencing a new program that places more emphasis on the clinical aspects of learning to teach. The students reported taking a similar set of university courses, but with more time in practical teaching experiences. In their third year, the students spend two months in an internship in a school and in their fourth year, the students work as a teaching assistant for one semester in a different school.

Teacher Certification Exams

Teachers must apply for a Teacher Qualification Certificate issued by the national government in order to be eligible to teach. Teachers can qualify for one of seven types of teaching certificates in China: kindergarten, primary school, junior secondary, senior secondary, secondary vocational, secondary vocational internship adviser, or higher education. These certificates also have a subject matter specialization based on the candidate's field of study.

Prior to 2014, candidates who attended a Normal School and completed a teacher preparation program could apply directly for the teaching certificate and were exempt from further certification examinations because it was assumed that they had the requisite knowledge and skills as a result of their program of study. Today, every teacher candidate must take the national certification exam.

The scope and content of certification exam was at one time set at the provincial level. Expectations for teachers were set lower in some regions in order to meet the demands for teachers in schools. A new national certification exam is now replacing the locally developed certification exams in a policy effort to raise the overall qualifications, and thus, quality, of the teaching force in China (Interview, Professor Ding Gang, November 2013). This new nationally standardized exam went into effect in 2013.

The exam comprises three parts. First the candidate must pass written examinations in pedagogy, psychology, and teaching methods. If the candidate is successful on these aspects of the examination, they then participate in an interview process with master teachers and local school district officials who themselves are typically former teachers. During this interview, the candidate demonstrates their teaching ability in specific subject matter instruction, shows their teaching process and handwriting skills on the blackboard, and may be asked about their classroom management and classroom questioning techniques. Finally, all teachers must also pass the Mandarin language test (with both speaking and listening components). Some special considerations in the passing scores are afforded to candidates who live in areas where Mandarin, the official language of China, is mixed with local dialects or other languages (Gang & Meilu, 2007).

In addition to the national certification exam, provinces can administer exams during the hiring process as Shanghai does. (See below.)

Recruiting and Hiring Teachers in Shanghai

Shanghai is not experiencing a shortage of qualified teaching candidates as a municipality and has a competitive market for teaching positions. Candidates from Shanghai Normal University reported that as Shanghai residents, they would apply for three to four teaching positions and secure a job rather quickly. The candidates prepared at East China Normal University who are not Shanghai residents and have a national scholarship will return to their home province to secure a job and those who choose to apply for a job in Shanghai will apply for positions at about 10 schools in order to secure a position. If they are offered a position, it will likely be in the outer-lying areas of the city where teaching positions are less competitive. Within Shanghai, there is a desire on the part of teachers to teach in districts within the city that offer higher salaries and have more high-performing schools. This results in a more competitive teaching market in the downtown and business districts in the city and less competition in the outer-lying districts and county within Shanghai municipality.

In an interview for this study with a principal in an outer-lying district, he described the difficulty he had maintaining qualified music teachers and that the selection pool he had for hiring in his school was not of the same high caliber as the pool for jobs in the more highly economically developed areas of Shanghai where there is more wealth and parental pressure for school quality. Research reports of case studies of schools in Shanghai also show that schools with higher migrant populations in Shanghai tend to have teachers who have lower qualifications than teachers in other schools (Wang & Holland, 2011).

Professor Wu Defang served as the Deputy Director of the Division of Schooling and Lifelong Education for East China Normal University in 2013–2014. She also works in Xuhui District in Shanghai specializing in teacher recruitment. In an interview with her, she described the process of candidate hiring. Every district has its own recruitment office and hiring office. The district administration knows the school-based needs for hiring teachers. Advertising, application, and hiring takes place at the district level and teachers are placed in the schools. An applicant should hold a teaching certificate which in most cases means they have completed a teacher training program and passed the national teacher exam. An example of a call for job applicants in Xuhui District in the city center is show in Figure 6.4. Note that in this call for applicants, one call is posted to fill 385 positions across kindergarten, elementary, secondary, and vocational schools. The hiring procedure includes a preliminary screening, comprehensive test on pedagogy and teaching, psychological exam, interview for overall quality, physical exam, and then hiring for those who make it through the entire process. This call for applicants also specifies an age range for the candidates, a practice that is not typical in the United States.

During the hiring process, the candidate is asked to take a written district-level exam. The district exams contain content knowledge questions, questions about other subject areas, and a few questions about

Figure 6.4 Job posting for teacher applicants in Xuhui District, Shanghai.

Xuhui School District Teacher recruitment ad for 2012 academic year

For an orderly operation of the teacher recruitment for the 2012 academic year, regulations are set up as follows:

1. Jobs
For open positions, please refer to Xuhui School district website — User service — Human Resources – Job list.

2. Candidates
1) College graduates of 2013; graduates from Normal University are preferred given everything else being equal;
2) Currently employed teachers;
3) Approximately 385 positions in total in Kindergarten, elementary, secondary, and vocational schools;

3. Requirements/qualifications
1) Have passion for education and obey the laws; Physically and mentally healthy and decent-looking; have required degrees and skills; excellent transcripts (for college graduates of the year). Currently employed teachers must have the title of level 1 secondary teacher or the award of lead teacher higher than school district level.
2) Age: college graduates must be under 30 years old; currently employed teachers under 45 years old.
3) Degree: At least college degrees for elementary and secondary teaching positions; At least associate degrees for kindergarten teaching positions.
4) Title: Currently employed teachers must have at least intermediate professional titles.
5) Certification: diploma, Teaching qualification certificate, professional expertise or title certificate, certificates in English language, computer, or other relevant areas; Kindergarten teacher candidates must have the certificate for pre-school teaching qualification.
6) Educational researchers: Must have at least college degree from non-normal universities, preferably superior/senior professional title at secondary level, at least 10 years teaching experience in the public school in the city, at the age of 40 years old or so. The candidate must demonstrate strong work capabilities, have relatively high reputation in the discipline, relatively strong teaching research abilities, relatively strong organization, planning, communication, and coordination abilities, and relatively strong language communication, writing, and information processing abilities.

4. Procedures
1) The employer unit conducts evaluations after a preliminary screening.
2) The employer unit recommends selected candidates to the Talents Service Center at the Education Bureau for a comprehensive test on pedagogy and teaching.

3) The candidates who pass the test take a psychological exam and an interview for overall quality.

4) The candidates who pass all the tests take the physical exam.

5) The candidates who pass the physical exam go through hiring procedures.

5. Application

1) On-site application

   a. November 2, 2012, Shanghai Winter Long Triangle Teacher recruitment session

   b. November 8, 2012, 2013 College Graduate Campus Recruitment in Shanghai Normal University (elementary teachers only)

   c. November 21, 2012, 2013 College Graduate Meeting session in East China Normal University, Campus Promotion Session

   d. December 14, 2012, 2013 College Graduate Large-Scale Campus Recruitment in Shanghai Normal University (normal universities only)

2) Online application

   Application materials will be uploaded at Xuhui School District Website (xhedu.sh.cn) — Human Resources — Talents recommendation, between November 7, 2012 and December 10, 2012.

3) Submission:

   For graduates of 2013: Recommendation form for graduates, transcripts, and other related certificates

   For currently employed teachers: Graduation certificate, Teaching qualification certificate, professional skill and/or title certificates, etc.

6. Contact

Address: Room 411, Yongjia Road 354, Talents Service Center, Xuhui School District Education Bureau, 200032

Phone: 54665871

Contact: Teacher Zang

7. Note

If qualified, the employer unit or the Talented Service Center in the Education Bureau will contact you. We apologize for not being able to respond to all the submissions.

Xuhui School District Bureau
October 2012

pedagogy. These exams are constructed by content area specialists on the district research staff. These staff members are typically highly respected teachers from within the district who are now working at the district level. Each subject area has a director, and this director will write questions for the exam, grade the exam, and participate in the interview process for the potential hire. The exams include both multiple choice and open-ended questions.

After passing the district-level exam, the candidate participates in an interview with a panel of experts in the content area from the district office. The interview questions can range from specific content knowledge questions, questions about how to teach particular concepts to students, and pedagogical questions such as "what do you think is most important in preparing a lesson?" In many interviews, the candidate is asked to teach a short lesson to the interview panel on a topic that the panel has selected.

Inducting Beginning Teachers in Shanghai

Based on my observation and analysis, I suggest that the induction of beginning teachers in China can be described through four perspectives: the policy perspective on supporting beginning teachers, the socialization of bringing beginning teachers into a professional community, the cultural expectation of experienced teachers assisting beginning teachers, and the evaluation perspective on the decision to rehire past the first year probation.

From a policy perspective, preservice teacher education in China primarily focuses on subject-specific content knowledge and basic knowledge of pedagogy through courses on psychology and teaching methods. Students in teacher education degree programs typically have 12 weeks total for practicum and student teaching experiences across their four years of college. To learn to manage classrooms and design instruction for large groups of students, the beginning teacher must receive a lot of early career support from the teachers within the school where he or she begins to teach. To ensure that this continued training happens systematically across the entire municipality, the Shanghai Municipal Education Commission created a formal induction policy in the late 1980s (International Alliance of Leading Education Institutes, 2008, p. 65).

The induction policy provides new teachers with a one-year probationary status. During this first year, all new teachers are assigned a mentor who is selected based on experience and reputation as a highly skilled teacher. This experienced colleague works closely with the new teacher, guiding them through processes such as lesson planning, selecting teaching materials and methods, decisions about student assignments, and giving feedback to students. The mentoring pair work together for a minimum of two hours per week (International Alliance of Leading Education Institutes, 2008, p. 65). Mentors also observe new teachers and new teachers are expected to observe their mentors in order to see models of highly skilled instruction. Mentors keep records of their activities and document the development of the beginning teachers for review by the school principal.

Given the school schedule structure, mentors have time in their contractual day to work with beginning teachers and to make these observations possible. In addition, mentors are also evaluated through feedback from the beginning teachers and the expectations that the school leaders have for the development of the beginning teacher (Salleh & Tan, 2013). Each school I visited also had a teacher serving as a professional learning coordinator who had responsibilities for structuring the mentoring pairs, organizing the teacher research meetings, and reporting to the district.

New teachers also have access to training provided by the Shanghai district in areas such as professional ethics, teaching theory, and teaching skills and are expected to participate in at least 30 hours of training (International Alliance of Leading Education Institutes, 2008, p. 65). For new teachers who did not have formal teacher preparation, the district offers four courses: pedagogy, psychology, subject-area methods, and *banzhuren* training.

From the socialization perspective, beginning teachers have close contact with experienced teachers on a regular basis through teacher study and research groups (see below for a description of the *jiaoyanzu*). Teachers begin to participate in joint lesson planning sessions and are observed by peers on a regular basis, not just for the purposes of formal evaluation but for the purposes of improving lesson design and hearing how experienced teachers think about instructional design and decisions. Participating in teacher working groups provides a method of socialization for new teachers into a community that shares a common body of knowledge, speaks a common language, and most importantly, shares a set of expectations for student performance and how to support them toward those goals.

From the cultural expectations of *lao dai qing*, translated as "the old bring along the young," are embedded in the work of teaching (Paine & Ma, 1993). This is apparent in how teachers talk about their commitment to their students and is also seen in the relationships between the experienced teachers and the beginning teachers.

> Central to this notion of *lao dai qing* is the idea of connectedness: The old and young are connected. Their connection comes through knowledge of and skill in teaching (as well as a commitment to that practice). In this we see a glimpse of a shared collectivist orientation. At the same time, there is an expectation of difference: that the older teachers, the *lao dai*, have something to offer the young, the *qing*.
>
> (Paine & Ma, 1993)

Finally, from an employment and evaluation perspective, the first year of teaching is a critical decision point for the hiring school and for the beginning teacher. At the end of the first year of teaching, teachers are assessed via written exams and based on the observations made at the school level by the mentor and the school principal. Those who do not meet the assessment standards at the end of the first year are either not rehired or are delayed from moving to permanent status. When rehired after their probation year, it is very rare for a teacher to be released from the job or fired. The majority of teachers are evaluated as having potential to succeed. According to a district deputy superintendent in Shanghai, about two to four teachers are dismissed from her district each year after their first year and after that, dismissal rarely occurs (Interview, Zhu Yue 26 November 2013). The teachers who are released, Zhu says, "are usually ones who have been pressed into becoming a teacher by their families and their heart is not in it." A journalist investigating Shanghai's education system described the rigorous evaluation processes for teachers and then concluded:

> That does not mean getting rid of poor teachers—something some education reformers in the U.S. argue is critical. In Shanghai, in fact, it's even more difficult to get rid of a bad teacher than it is in most urban systems in the U.S. "Basically," one Shanghai principal says, "they have to commit some sort of crime" to be dismissed.
>
> (Burningham, 2014)

According to Gu Lingyuan, Head of the China Centre for Research on Teacher Continuing Education, the induction practices in China have enabled a majority of teachers to make an effective transition into classroom teaching, yet not all will go on to become a master teacher.

Salleh and Tan (2013) identified three key strengths in how Shanghai implements its mentoring system. First, the centralized education system of China creates a system that is not only well defined, but is held in regard for compliance by the teachers and school leaders. Rather than being a coercive device, Salleh and Tan argue that this required system "corresponds to the Asian cultural values of respect for authority and conformity" (p. 157) and thus the accountability and inspection that are embedded in the mentoring process become levers for ensuring that the mentoring framework is fully implemented at the local level. Second, they conclude that the mentoring system is based on sound pedagogical principles of teacher learning including the collaborative and collective nature of learning that occurs. Third, they describe the mentoring process as focused on actual classroom teaching as seen in the requirements for observation and feedback and the focus on lesson design and student assignments. But the system does not go without critique from these authors. They also point out that the value of education for Shanghai students and parents is often instrumental (toward successful careers) rather than intrinsic (toward learning) and that this is supported by the value placed on examinations and prestige. Within this culture, mentoring beginning teachers is trapped in a cycle of reproducing the existing values. In a similar vein, the authors point out that beginning teachers have little status to be able to question or challenge the more experienced teachers given the value that is placed on expertise and the hierarchical systems within schools. Without a voice, the beginning teachers' ideas and innovation can be stifled amid the traditions and know-how of the selected mentors.

7

SUPPORTING TEACHER PROFESSIONAL LEARNING IN SHANGHAI

IN CHINA, TEACHERS ENGAGE in ongoing professional learning in six ways. First, they are required to document their participation in training opportunities for a specified amount of time; second, they participate in subject specific study and research groups; third, they participate in cross-disciplinary or grade level study groups; fourth, teachers conduct peer observations in their own school and in other schools; fifth, they actively conduct research on teaching; and sixth, they participate in teaching competitions. Each of these modes of teacher professional learning will be discussed in turn in the first section that follows. Subsequently, I will discuss career ladders and leadership opportunities for teachers and then conclude this section with a brief description of how teachers are compensated and evaluated.

Teacher Professional Learning in Shanghai

First, according to the MOE's Regulations for the Continuing Education of Primary and Secondary School Teachers (1999), teachers must participate in ongoing learning opportunities in the following areas: political education and the ethics of teaching, subject matter specialization, current educational theory and practice, teaching schools, and educational technologies. All teachers are required to participate in a minimum of 240 hours (a professional development hour is equivalent to 45 minutes of clock time) of trainings every five years.

These workshops and classes are offered by the school districts and in partnership with higher education campuses. In a national survey of teachers about their professional development experiences, teachers

Table 7.1 Organizing agencies of teaching activities participated in
by teachers.

Rank/Order	Organizing Agencies	Percentage (%)
1	Non-normal universities	61.4
2	Other	47.0
3	Specialized skill-training institutes	36.4
4	Upper-rank education administration institutes	31.1
5	Colleges of education/teacher training schools	30.4
6	Never participated in any training	4.1
7	In the school	3.6
8	Normal universities	3.0

Note: This is a multiple choice item and more than one answer was allowed,
thus the percentage total is more than 100%.
Source: (Gang, 2010, p. 172, Table 9–1)

reported a fairly even distribution of participating in professional development programming offered by specialized skill-training institutes that
are usually sponsored by the district, upper-rank education administration institutes that are usually sponsored by the province (or in the case
of Shanghai, the municipality), and colleges of education (see Table 7.1).

Second, teachers regularly participate in a *jiaoyanzu*, which translates
to "teaching research group." The *jiaoyanzu* are formal organizational
units in schools across China. In comparison to the United States, the
jiaoyanzu look like a subject matter department unit—a group of math
teachers or a group of English teachers. At the senior secondary level,
the *jioyanzu* may also include other school personnel such as laboratory
assistants. But because teachers in China are all specialized in their subject
area, *jiaoyanzu* exist in primary schools and junior secondary schools as
well. Typically, *jiaoyanzu* have three to eight teachers, depending on the
size of the school. The members of the *jiaoyanzu* share office space with
one another and hold their meetings in school conference rooms.

Jiaoyanzu are led by a teacher who is recognized in the school as a
very good teacher. This teacher will have been advanced up the rank
ladder (described below) or have been recognized with teaching awards.
It is also possible for a promising younger teacher to be identified as
the head of a *jiaoyanzu*, thus providing a distinction among teachers
that distinguishes teachers based on their teaching skill and professional
performance. The school principal works closely with the heads of the
jiaoyanzu who serve as an informal council or cabinet for advising the
principal. *Jiaoyanzu* are so common in China, they go unnoticed within
the country as something worth describing in the research and policy

literature: "Working together constitutes the circumstances or environment in which Chinese teachers work; like the air in which we live, it seems to be too common and too customary for people to notice its existence" (Paine & Ma, 1993, p. 677).

Jiaoyanzu typically meet on a weekly basis and engage in a variety of activities as part of their responsibilities to one another and other teachers. The goal of the *jiaoyanzu* is the improvement of educational practices for individual teachers as well as the school. To accomplish this goal, the *jiaoyanzu* members participate in a variety of activities that are directly connected to curriculum, teaching, and student learning. Their activities may include, but are not limited to, examining curriculum together, designing lessons, observing each other teach and discussing the lesson together, writing tests, coordinating teacher professional development such as lectures and visit to other schools, working with student teachers from preparation programs, soliciting input from students on the quality of teaching they are experiencing, and looking at student work.

Paine and Ma (1993) have described how the *jiaoyanzu* structure in Chinese schools creates an expectation of joint or collective work and decision making for teachers and establishes a different set of expectations for the daily work of teaching in China when compared to US schools:

> While the teacher is still the person chiefly responsible for classroom teaching, many decisions about curriculum and instruction are made jointly through the *jiaoyanzu*. In this sense, the teacher's field is narrower and more focused than it might be in a U.S. setting. At the same time, because of the presence of the teaching research group, the teacher's role is broader. That is, rather than being chiefly a classroom teacher, the teacher is also a teacher educator—working with colleagues (experienced and new) to educate each other about teaching—as well as researcher or inquirer into teaching, curriculum, and learning. While U.S. teachers are increasingly identified as having these roles, the Chinese organizational context has long made these functions of teaching visible in and central to a teacher's daily tasks. (p. 679)

Third, teachers also participate in smaller, grade level, lesson planning groups called *beikezu*. These groups run much like the *jiaoyanzu*, but have a particular focus on lesson planning and focus on bringing the curriculum to the appropriate grade level of the student. The work of these groups reflects a more recent phenomenon of focusing on the child as learner and trying to make curriculum and instruction more learner-centered.

Fourth, teachers conduct peer observations in their own school and in other schools. In many respects, teaching is a collective activity in China (Paine & Ma, 1993) built on the premise that the pooling together of good ideas and resources will reflect well on the school, not the individual, and better serve the students in that school. Teachers in China share a long tradition of planning together and observing each other's lessons. Teaching is not a private activity in China as it is perceived in some other cultures and the practice of peer observation is referred to "open class-room" (Interview, Gu Zhiyue, 3 December 2013). In a national survey of teachers about their professional learning activities, 57% reported that they had participated in classroom observations, teaching competition, and other teaching research activities in the past two years (See Figure 7.1).

During school site visits in Shanghai, I observed teachers in *jiaoyanzu* and *beikezu* meetings at three different schools. In each school, the teachers brought forward lesson plans for discussion, then taught the lesson

Figure 7.1 Proportion of teachers' participation in training forms and professional development in the past two years

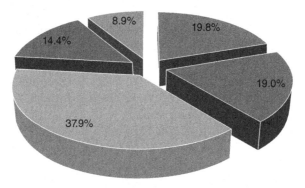

- Training, lectures, organized by universities or other training institutes
- Classroom observation, teaching competition, and other teaching-research activities in other schools
- Classroom observation, teaching competition, and other teaching-research activities in the school
- Teaching or subject-area seminar, conference, training (not including regular teaching-research activities in the school)
- Other

Gang, 2010, p. 171, Figure 9–2.

in her classroom while other teachers and administrators observed, and then the group debriefed the lesson to give feedback on how to improve the lesson (Figure 7.2). The feedback discussion followed a common structure. The teacher gave some opening comments about the lesson and a summary of how they thought the lesson went. The group leader, typically the most senior teacher, then provided a few comments on what the lesson did successfully and then gave one or two suggestions for improvement. A few other teachers would then follow suit, give a summary of what they thought went well and some suggestions for improvement. If a principal or other higher ranked person was participating, they gave a longer summary at the end of the conversation, inserting some broader commentary about the kind of teaching the school should be striving toward. Otherwise, the leader of the group would provide a summary of the comments. These meetings lasted the same duration as a typical school class period—about 35 minutes.

As a US-based outsider, I was struck in these discussions by the level of detail that was discussed in the post-observation meetings. In one meeting, a teacher made a suggestion for changing the specific words on a PowerPoint slide and in another meeting, a principal commented on the precision of the teacher language in teaching a math lesson. This illustrates to me the care and precision in which the lesson design is

Figure 7.2 Teacher study group conducting a post-lesson discussion with professors from East China Normal University, Pujian No. 2 Elementary School, Shanghai.

conceived in China. I was also struck by the overall press for giving the students more time for independent work during the lessons. The lessons, however, were already quite dense in their content and activity, making providing more time for students to talk and work a challenge without removing something else from the lesson content. Suggestions for what to remove were not discussed. This illustrates to me how teachers live in ongoing tension turning the time over to the students while not letting go of their duty to provide deep content information. Finally, I was struck by the directness of the commentary from teachers and administrators and how little reflection and thinking about the substance of these suggestions was expected of the demonstrating teacher during the meeting. In much professional development in the United States, we try to practice a reflective stance in mentoring by asking the teacher questions and listening to their reflections. When I noted this observation to the teachers, they said they would take all of the new ideas they received and reflect on them later individually and then they would choose what advice to implement and what suggestions to leave alone.

When creating a lesson for a peer observation, teachers complete a lesson plan. The lesson plan format is typically school-based. In the sample lesson plan outline in Figure 7.3 we can see that the lesson is

---

Figure 7.3 Sample lesson planning outline from Shanghai.

I.   Unit objectives

II.   Lesson objectives

Class 1	
Class 2	

III. Lesson plan for Class 1

1. Teaching objectives
2. Rationales for objectives
   1) Textbook analysis
   2) Student analysis
      a. Knowledge evaluation
      b. Proficiency evaluation
      c. Difficulty analysis

situated within an overall unit of study. The objectives for the lesson may vary from one class to the next. This is a good reminder that the class in China is a group of students that stays together so each class may have its own needs in terms of pacing the learning and how to focus the lesson. The teacher is expected to think through her decisions and rationales for why and how she will teach the lesson in advance. This lesson analysis includes the teachers' reasoning behind what is being taught (textbook analysis), what she expects the students to learn and at what depth (knowledge and proficiency evaluation), and what she anticipates the students having difficulty with during the lesson (difficulty analysis).

As stated before, teaching in China is an open and publicly examined practice. This openness creates a stronger collective set of ideals for which to gauge strong teaching versus weak teaching. It is still up to the individual teacher to execute lessons and manage large groups of students in tight-fitting classrooms. However, the individual holds images of "good teaching" and the drive toward individual improvement by being immersed in an overall culture that allows him or her to see colleagues perform on a regular basis.

> Given frequent peer observation and joint preparation, Chinese teachers are well informed about the teaching quality of their colleagues in the whole school and are able to make comments on colleagues' teaching style, subject knowledge level, capacity for managing class discipline, strength and weakness in teaching, and reputation among students. They are proud of good teachers in the school and feel sorry for some colleagues who have trouble in teaching. Outstanding teachers are respected among their colleagues for their excellent teaching rather than their personality.
>
> (Paine & Ma, 1993, p. 682)

Fifth, teachers actively participate in research on teaching. This research is not perceived as a one-off project to fulfill a degree requirement or to complete a program. Teachers are taught in their preparation programs about research methods and how to think through a research problem, and throughout their careers, they conduct research on their teaching and their schools. This research is often conducted in small groups and the *jiaoyanzu* is a key place for this to take place. Teachers also do their own research individually (Liang et al., 2012). During interviews for this study teachers made reference to their research and what they had learned. Schools annually file some of their research reports with their district office and much teacher research is published in books

Table 7.2 Teachers' research and publications.

	Number of people (n)	Percentage (%)
Never published	2869	25.6
1–3 publications	4801	42.9
4–6 publications	2029	18.1
7–9 publications	603	5.4
More than 9 publications	887	7.9

Source: (Gang, 2010, p.148, Table 7–2).

and teaching magazines. In a national survey of teachers, about 75% of the respondents (N =11,189) reported having at least one publications of their own research (Table 7.2).

Some teachers hold the title of researching teacher and have positions in the district offices. These teachers help coordinate and monitor the research happening in schools. Topics of research range from pedagogical issues, subject-matter specific questions, administration processes, and educational policies. Teachers give most attention to subject-matter specific questions (see Figure 7.4).

The sixth and final approach to ongoing professional learning of teachers is their participation in local, district, and state level teaching

Figure 7.4 Distribution of research projects contents above school level

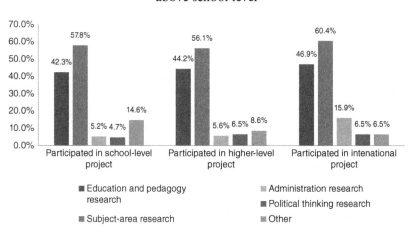

Gang, 2010, p. 147, Figure 7–2.

Figure 7.5 Teaching competition photo posted by a teacher on WeChat, a social networking platform in China.

competitions on a regular basis. The teaching competitions require a teacher to conduct a lesson in front of a panel of judges and receive a rating on an observation protocol. The lesson plan for that lesson is also made available to the judges so that they can see how the teacher reasoned about their selection of teaching strategies and student engagement strategies.

Teaching competitions and demonstrations at provincial and national levels are open events with many observers and do not necessarily take place in a classroom. In Figure 7.5, a classroom has been set up in an auditorium to allow for judges and observers to participate. In school settings, open classroom sessions look similar with several adult observers pressed against the walls of the classroom while the teacher conducts a lesson.

Lessons for teaching competitions are rated using an evaluation form. The sample evaluation form in Figure 7.6 illustrates the type of teacher-student interactions that are expected during well-designed lessons. Teachers must demonstrate that they can attend to the content they are teaching, the methods they use, and to the students' engagement in the lesson.

Figure 7.6 Qibao Experimental Middle School "Rigorous Classroom Teaching Expert" Teaching Contest Evaluation Form.

Grade		Subject		Project		
Teacher		Years of teaching		Title /rank		Other responsibilities /jobs

Evaluation categories	Evaluation content	Evaluation items	Evaluation results (Please tick √ the one that fits)			
			Excellent	Relatively good	Average	Relatively poor
Teacher behaviors	Teaching content	1. Teaching content is effective and reasonable; teaching objectives is appropriate for the context.				
		2. Lesson plan design is an organic component of the curriculum, emphasizes integration with other knowledge, and is connected to the school context.				
	Teaching methods	3. The instruction reflects the learning-before-teaching theory; there is a scientific and effective instructional support for learning.				
		4. The teacher respects, motivates, and appreciates students; the teacher gives timely feedback and uses quantifiable evaluation for students' group performance.				
		5. The teacher guides, prompts, inspires, and challenges students responsively and appropriately; there is timely and appropriate feedback and adjustment.				

Category	Criteria
	6. The teacher attends to all students and differentiates instruction according to individuals; the teacher cares for struggling students and uses various ways to involving them in learning.
Learning	7. Classroom dynamic is good; students are engaged and energetic.
	8. It includes diversified ways of learning; it involves independent, explorative, and cooperative learning.
	9. The majority of the students are engaged; no students is off task; more than 80% is in a good learning condition.
Student behaviors	10. Group work is used in a meaningful way and has a strong connection with learning content.
	11. The time spent on exploration, cooperation, presentation, and communication takes up to more than 80%; it's clearly student-centered.
Learning effects	12. Most students can reach the learning goals, have a good grasp of key learning contents, and make progress in challenging areas.
	13. Students at all levels have successful learning experiences; struggling students participate in learning and are not off task.
Overall evaluation	Positives and analysis:
	Major areas for improvements and analysis:

The evaluation shows us what is considered not only good, but award-winning teaching in Shanghai. First, content knowledge should be accurate, meaningful, and there should be a strong rationale for how it is appropriate for the teaching context. The instructional expectations are many-faceted. The lesson should show how the teacher is building on what the students have learned prior to this particular lesson. The teachers' role is to encourage and motivate, to guide, prompt, and inspire the students during the lesson. The lesson evaluation gives explicit attention not only to teaching practices, but also calls out how to design the lesson with learning in mind. The student-centered nature of instruction is quantified, with 80% of the lesson designed for exploration, cooperation, presentation, and communication. Broad-based student engagement is expected, with attention to all the students regardless of their performance standing in the class. For example, in lesson observations conducted for this study, teachers used a variety of tracking techniques during the lesson to help them know how many and which students participated in the lesson. Lessons had a high degree of interaction between the teacher and the students through questioning, call and response with the whole class, paired conversations between the students, student's demonstrating their work on chalkboards, students showing their work with simple math manipulatives and demonstration materials they brought from home.

Finally, teaching is viewed as having learning effects—with most students reaching the learning goals and all students staying engaged and having a good learning experience. The overall evaluation section illustrates the structure of the feedback I observed in the in *jiaoyanzu* and *beikezu* meetings I observed. The teachers receive some general summary comments in a positive vein and then some suggestions for how to improve the lesson.

In summary, teachers learning from teachers is the norm in China. It is also the most highly valued form of learning by teachers. In a national survey of teachers about their professional learning activities, teachers reported that experienced teachers, colleagues teaching the same grade level, and colleagues teaching the same subject had a larger impact on their professional learning than school leaders, experts outside of the school, or students did (see Figure 7.7).

Career Ladders and Leadership for Teachers

Four approaches to teacher advancements and leadership opportunities can be teased out of the varied ways in which teachers are recognized and awarded in China. Chinese teachers have an explicit

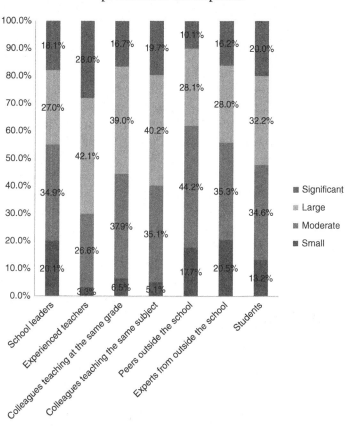

Figure 7.7 Different people's impact on teacher professional development

Gang, 2010, p. 201, Figure 10–7.

career ladder of advancement based on their professional knowledge, skills, and accomplishments. They also hold an implicit recognition of accomplished peers through cultural and social status afforded to those who hold great respect from others. Accomplished teachers in China are often rewarded and publicly recognized for their knowledge, skills, and accomplishments. And finally, some teachers choose to take career advancement from the classroom into school administration and district level roles and responsibilities. Each of these is described in turn.

First, teachers in China are formally classified into four "grades" or ranks: probationary status, second level, first level, and senior teacher. They progress from one grade to the next based on their professional competence and status among their peers. To be promoted on the rank scale, the teachers are required to do many things such as write a summary about their work in the past few years, take written tests to show their language competence, write research papers on teaching, participate in interviews held by the district, and be observed by experienced teachers. Moving up the rank ladder for a teacher brings about a sense of professional accomplishment and pride. Teachers in a school readily know the grade category of other teachers and think of higher ranked teachers as mentors and school leaders. For example, the head of a *jiaoyanzu* will frequently be an experienced and accomplished teacher of a higher rank. Lower rank teachers are typically beginning their careers.

 To advance from one rank to the next, teachers submit an application at the district level (Link 7-1). Applications typically include the teachers' current rank and all degrees they hold, an overview of school-based research work in which they are currently engaged, a list of awards and prizes, and recognition of students' accomplishments, and a list of published research and papers. The school must approve the application first, which typically means the principal is in agreement that the teacher has the qualifications to apply. At the district level, a committee of experts—typically subject area coordinators or teacher professional development staff who themselves have been recognized for their accomplished teaching—review the applications and make the decision about rank advancement.

The district limits the number of teachers they advance to higher ranks, which increases the competitiveness of a successful application. The national distribution of teachers across these ranks is represented in Figure 7.8. Here, we see that the Senior titled teachers comprise an elite group with only 6.6% of the teachers overall holding this rank. It is also interesting to note that the high schools (senior secondary schools) have the highest percentage of senior-ranked teachers. These teachers likely hold higher degrees than the middle school teachers.

In cases of little rank advancement by an experienced teacher, the highly ranked teachers are often called upon to support and guide those teachers to assist in their improvement process. Professional learning opportunities for teachers are also structured for the different teacher rank levels to support them in moving up a career ladder. The principal of an elementary school in Shanghai described these opportunities as

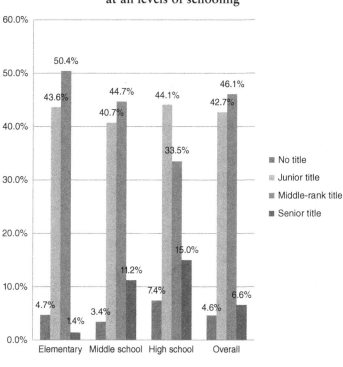

Figure 7.8 Teachers' professional titles
at all levels of schooling

Gang, 2010, p. 14, Figure 7.

occurring at the school level, the district level, and then the municipal level in Shanghai:

> First, it sets up a platform for the school, which means offering opportunities for the teachers, to grow, to have space. Then, if you have several years of teaching experiences in the school and you are accomplished, then you have the opportunity to participate in district-level professional trainings for lead teachers. In the training, you could learn more through research projects and with guidance from experts of all sorts. Next, you will have the opportunity to attend trainings at the municipal level. At this level, there is a dual opportunity to learn—with teachers and with other schools—where you could obtain a more professional and focused support in learning. Such a space for growth actually is a strong incentive for teachers who see the possibility of being promoted step by step. Besides the regular award system like senior instructor system in elementary and

secondary schools, the professional development opportunities serves as a great platform for teachers to advance in their work.

(principal interview, Jiansulu Primary School, Shanghai)

The second way in which teachers gain and take on leadership is through implicitly recognized distinctions among teachers. The informal identification of teachers as "backbone teachers" in the *jiaoyanzu* is an example of this within the culture of teaching in China. Paine and Ma (1993) describe backbone teachers as:

> Those who are more active in the activities of the *jiaoyanzu* and have a good reputation in teaching . . . backbone teachers contribute much to what and how the group works to improve its teaching quality. In effect they operate as assistants and resource people for the group head. When the group sets up a new program, typically they are the ones who will try it first. They also mentor or coach new teaches. If we think of the *jiaoyanzu* as a substantial level in the organization of a school, a backbone teacher should be seen as a substantial component of the group. (p. 680)

To some, the structure of the career ladder in China may seem hierarchical. To a large extent, there is a clear status difference in *jiaoyanzu* meetings, with less-experienced teachers serving tea, not speaking as much as more-experienced teachers, and sitting on the periphery. The head of the *jiaoyanzu* takes a central seat at the conference table, is the first person to provide feedback on a lesson, and summarizes all the feedback at the end of the meeting. Yet, the status differential does not put the more experienced teachers in a position of authority or leader. Liping Ma (Paine & Ma, 1993) summarized the relational elements among teachers in these groups as follows:

> Featuring Chinese teachers' working together, it is easy for one to see that they do not work in a democratic way. The principle of one person, one vote is not applied there. However, it seems not to be a static hierarchy either. A teaching research group leader or a backbone teacher does not have any legal authority. Their prestige does not allow them to dictate what another teacher must do. Such a teacher is considered an expert rather than a leader. Others will take advantage of their expertise as resources, rather than be passively directed by another teacher. The experts are at the center of an eddy rather than at the top of a ladder. (p. 689)

The third way that teachers in China are advanced in their career is through public recognition of awards and accomplishments. Teachers'

Figure 7.9 Award-winning teachers
in public display at Qibao Experimental
Middle School, Shanghai.

awards are communicated to the school community through the cele-
bration of teachers' accomplishments by the school principal. In three
schools I visited for this study, photos and accomplishments of teachers
were posted in the school hallways and on marquees that stand outside
of the school buildings (Figures 7.9 and 7.10). These awards add prestige
to the whole school community.

Figure 7.10 Award-winning teachers in school
display at Pujian No. 2 Elementary School, Shanghai.

Finally, advancing to higher levels of educational administration in schools, district offices, city commissions, and national ministry is also based on one's career accomplishments as a teacher.

> Almost all the officers in the government education authorities, both at municipal and district levels, started as school teachers. Most of them distinguished themselves as teachers or school principals with strong track records. This perhaps explains their devoted professional attention to teaching and learning amidst all the administrative chores and political issues they normally contend with. They manage, however, to maintain this teaching focus while at the same time relying on a strategic vision that enables them to navigate a policy arena which goes well beyond education.
>
> (OECD, 2010, p. 89)

School principals encountered in this study had achieved the highest rank as a teacher and talked proudly about their teaching accomplishments. They tended to link what they know about successful teaching to how they provided guidance to their school staff and set a direction for the improvement of their school.

Teacher Compensation and Evaluation

Teachers in China have seen a dramatic increase in salaries and professionalization since the mid-1990s when the Teachers Law was enacted. Salaries prior to this law were very low, estimated as less than $10 USD per month. The law then stipulated that teachers were to be paid no less than other civil servants. Salaries have steadily increased since then, but gaps still exist. Two types of pay gaps exist for Chinese teachers. There is a steep divide in salaries between teachers in the western part of the country and teachers in the eastern regions. There is also a salary gap between teachers responsible for teaching mathematics, Chinese, social sciences, and sciences (the core curricular subjects which are tested) and those in the nontested subjects (e.g., art, music, physical education).

In general, teacher salaries in China are low relative to other professional occupations in China (Ingersoll, 2007). However, teaching is considered a very stable and respected career. In Shanghai, teachers' salaries are among the highest in the nation, estimated between 6000–10,000 Yuan ($960–1640 USD) per month. Salaries in other parts of China fall in a range of 3000–5000 Yuan per month ($480–800 USD). Teachers often subsidize their school-based salary through private tutoring and giving talks. While it is illegal in Shanghai and not spoken of publicly, collecting sponsoring fees from students who come from other neighborhoods or whose test scores are below the official admissions cut-off for the school is still practiced secretly by some.

Since 2009, China has been using a merit pay system for allocating teachers' salaries. The rationale for instituting a merit pay system has been publicly described as an effort to bring greater salary parity among teachers and to be fair in rewarding exemplary teachers. Before 2009, teachers' salaries had two parts: a base salary based on the teachers' professional rank and teaching experience and bonuses. The new merit pay system now requires districts to keep the average salary of all the teachers above the average salary of all public servants in the same district (in accordance with the Teacher Law of 1993), ensure that the salary is 70% base salary and 30% pay based on performance, and eliminates school bonuses. Prior to the merit pay system, teachers were regularly evaluated through annual evaluations and their applications to move up the teacher ranks. The merit pay system was intended make the salary awards for teachers more systematically and fairly applied.

For example, base salary is distributed to teachers primarily based on the number of classes they teach and the additional tasks and responsibilities that the teacher takes on. This might include being the *banzhuren* for a class, being the head of the *jiaoyanzu*, or conducting demonstration lessons for colleagues in the school or at other schools. The teacher is being paid for the actual work they do. Teachers are assigned the classes they teach by the school principal and the merit pay system has not had an impact on the number of class assignments a teacher has.

In Shanghai, the merit salary system is administered at the school level with oversight by the districts. The evaluation process and allocation of merit salary varies from school to school. Based on interviews during my visit to Shanghai, it is clear that evaluating teachers is a multifaceted process that does not rely on specific metrics of weighted formulas in order to determine the merit salary allocation for individual teachers. Principals rely on many different sources of information and indicators of success (Link 7-2), including performance of the teachers' students and professional advancements that the teacher makes. For example, when ninth graders test for their high school placement, teachers' pay can be linked to the success of their class based on student placement into prestigious schools. The merit salary of a *banzhuren* can be based on the exam performance of the class they direct. Teachers can also receive merit salary if their students perform well in academic competitions. In addition, principals observe teachers teach, they look at teachers' contributions to the development of new teachers, they look at teachers' publications and awards. They also consider the teachers' general reputation among their colleagues for their professionalism and dedication to advancing educational reforms.

Teachers and principals interviewed for this study did not place much value or importance on the merit pay systems. In interviews and focus groups, most teachers were not sure about how the merit system actually worked, although they clearly had a sense of who the more skillful teachers were in their building because they are the ones who demonstrate lessons and lead their study groups. The introduction of merit pay has made the evaluation process frustrating for some principals. The principal at Pujiang No. 2 Elementary School described how the evaluation approach is not specific enough to administer based on detailed differences among his teachers, so he relies on his knowledge of teachers' skill to group teachers in three big categories to make the salary system merit based.

> It is the toughest when it comes to performance incentives. . . The performance evaluation system we use includes formative evaluation, midterm evaluation, and final evaluation. The rationales behind these evaluations are not of high quality. In particular situations when some teachers' performance are close in evaluation. For example, Teacher Li is outstanding whereas the performance evaluation for you and me is close. But there should be some differences between our performance evaluations. This is the toughest part of the work, right? So the key issue is designing an evaluation system to the greatest details takes time and effort, which we don't have; the evaluation system that is broad and general fails to capture differences between teachers. . .What is your decision based on?. . . We cannot afford the time and effort to designing an evaluation system to the greatest details; we won't be able to have a solid base for incentives if the evaluation system is broad and general. So what we do now is global evaluation. In Chinese language arts, for example, we first determine who are the best teachers and then the worst. What is left is pretty much those in the middle. This way is efficient and it sounds fair. You are placed in the top/first rank whereas I am in the second as I should be. If one's teaching performance is apparently worse than others, or one breaks some minor regulation, they are downgraded.
>
> (Interview, principal of Piajian No. 2 Elementary School, November 2013)

A Shanghai teacher described the annual evaluation process in her school and suggested that her salary is not affected very much by the merit review:

> Teachers are required to write a summary about their work, and the principal and the other teachers evaluate his or her work according

to the summary. In most schools, teachers are also evaluated according to their teaching. His or her lessons are observed by the *jiaoyanzu zhang* (leader of teaching and research team) and other teachers and the students are required to fill in some evaluation forms. The result will be fed back to the teacher and sent to the principal, but not the district office. It does not make a huge difference in the salary, but helps the principle to decide which teachers can shoulder more important responsibility.

This quote also points out that student feedback is a routine part of the evaluation process for teachers. Schools and the district administer surveys to students and parents as part of the school evaluation process and questions about the teacher and classroom operations are reviewed by the principal. Questions on an annual student survey for Qilun Elementary School in Shanghai included (Link 7-3):

○ Who is your favorite male teacher? And/or who is your favorite female teacher?
○ Who is full of goodwill among your teachers?
○ Which subject do you like best in your curriculum? Who teaches (taught) this subject?
○ If you face difficulties in life or study, who will you seek for help?
○ Up till now, which teacher do you think helps you a lot in life or study?
○ In addition to those academic lessons, such as Chinese, Math and English, which subject do you like most? Who is the teacher?

These survey results are used in the principal judgment when making evaluation and merit pay decisions about a teacher.

A study conducted in Beijing after the merit pay system was implemented found that, overall, teachers' average pay was increased with the new system while some teachers experienced a decrease in salary (including in the academically prestigious schools). The study also found that the merit pay system was not a motivating program for teachers to perform differently than they had in the past (Niu & Liu, 2012).

8

CONCLUSION: HOW TEACHING CULTURE, POLICIES, AND PRACTICES SUPPORT STUDENT PERFORMANCE

THIS STUDY BEGAN BY ASKING how Shanghai's educational system—its culture, policies, and practices—is set up to support the kind of student performance we saw in the Shanghai PISA results. In particular, how does the system structure teaching, and the role and quality of teachers, to contribute to these outcomes? In this final summary I cannot draw causal conclusions between particular aspects of the Shanghai education system and the student exam performance. Throughout this study, I have tried to be descriptive to establish what the policy conditions in Shanghai look like, from national education law under which Shanghai is governed, to local practices of *jiaoyanzu* meetings and teaching competitions. In this summary, I will explore how culture, policy, and practice shape the work of Shanghai's teachers in an effort to answer the question of how the system supports teachers and student learning. I first look at the culture of respect for teachers and how it is reflected in China's educational policy and school practices. I then look at the educational policy and comment on the consistency in how the policies support the development of teachers. Finally, I turn to practice and reflect on how the daily work of teachers creates tightly choreographed lessons and practice-based research. I close with a brief reflection on how culture, policy, and practice influence classroom instruction and student learning and the tensions that the Chinese educational system is currently experiencing as policy shifts are trying to effect change in culture and practice.

Teachers in China, and Shanghai in particular, enjoy high status and great respect within the cultural traditions of the nation. This cultural respect is then reflected in policy and practices that define what teaching is, how the nation should support teachers, and how teaching expertise is called upon for school governance and reform activities. We see this respect inscribed in the national laws that iterate and reiterate the requirement for all sectors from grassroots to national financing to step up in support of teachers. We see this respect in the way parents and families hold high expectations for their children and, in turn, entrust teachers to provide the necessary support for their child's success. We see this respect in how school leadership is drawn from among the highest ranks of teachers and subsequently these principals rely on their teaching staff to guide the performance of the school as a whole. And finally, we see this respect in how school reform efforts in Shanghai turn to teachers and principals to provide expertise and guidance in how to turn around low-performing schools. Culturally, teachers are the backbone of the educational system in Shanghai.

When we examine the educational policy in China and Shanghai, we see that national policy has systematically supported the development of teachers for 30 years. From the beginning of compulsory education in 1986, to the Teachers' Law in 1995, through the educational reform laws of the 2006, and in the current 2020 Plan teachers have been identified as a cornerstone of educational success for students. The national government has called for increasing support for higher teacher salaries, better living conditions, stronger preparation, ongoing learning opportunities, and establishing awards to recognize teachers' accomplishments. In policies and reform plans that aim to improve the educational system, the focus is on national investments in teaching quality, and not on blaming teachers for school failure; on improvement rather than punishment or sanctions; and on deepening the pedagogical skills and repertoires of teachers to encourage innovative and creative thinking in their students rather than on improving test scores.

When we examine more local policy, such as how the school day is structured, how teachers spend their time, and how they are evaluated, we see a schooling system that is built on the concept that teachers' work is not only time in front of a classroom full of students. Instructional time is sacred in Shanghai schools. In order to create highly engaged lessons and the maximum learning opportunity for students, the school system allows time for deep and collaborative planning to design, execute, and redesign lessons. Teachers' expertise and experience is valued within the policies that have grown up around the requirement for new teacher mentoring and in how principals rely on a cabinet of the *jiaoyanzu zhang* (leader of teaching and research team) to provide leadership and guidance within the school. When teachers are evaluated, their work must show not only how they have contributed to the achievement and success of their students; they are also expected to contribute to the growth and development of other teachers and to the continual renewal of the schooling system. Teachers have a clearly defined career ladder to climb which brings with it recognition for their accomplishments, increased status among their peers, and leadership opportunities within their school and in other educational bureaus and commissions. The differentiated roles for teachers and the leadership opportunities that the career ladder affords supports the national policy call for teachers to be professionals who strive for lifelong learning and who contribute to improvement of the educational systems in which they work. These expectations are not trivial. They are inscribed in national law, built into the teachers' work day, and used to evaluate the performance of the teacher for movement up the ranks of the career ladder.

I think it is interesting that a merit-based evaluation and salary system introduced from the West into the Chinese context has frustrated school principals and has had little consequence for teachers. Of course teachers want to earn a good salary. But incentivizing teachers with a system of payment based on working hours and student achievement does not begin to capture the underlying value of the work that teachers perform on a regular basis. Teachers in Shanghai have been part of a system that expects them to build and reform the system from within through their collegial collaborations and how they "bring up" the next generation of teachers through mentoring and coaching. Most teachers feel a duty and responsibility to engage in ongoing improvement efforts and the highest performing ones are rewarded with professional respect, prestige, and recognition for their career contributions. These rewards are much more important than a salary formula to teachers who are passionate about their work and want to give back to those who come after them.

Teachers' school-based practices in China, and particularly in Shanghai, shape their work in important ways. These practices can only exist because of the policy supports that surround them—allowance of time, structured systems that organize the work, expectations of the work, and evaluation policies that lead to recognition for the work. Within the policy structure, the teachers create practices that reify local expectations. For example, lessons for teachers in Shanghai are critical to student engagement so teachers regularly collaborate on lesson design and observe each other to see models of effective instruction and give feedback to each other. Teachers' reputation and honor are enhanced by being recognized by their peers as being master teachers, so teachers publish research, give speeches, and are generally viewed as moral agents who set a model example of contribution to the collective good and as public intellectuals who represent the quality of the schooling system. Evaluation of teachers continues to rest on the teachers' accomplishments both in terms of student achievement and their contributions to improving teaching and learning, even in light of new policy efforts to base pay more precisely on performance. These local practices reflect the cultural expectations in China while being supported by the way the system of schooling has been established through policy.

I cannot directly address the underlying question on the minds of Western policy makers: why do Shanghai students perform so well on the international PISA exams? But I can suggest that the culture, policy, and practices that surround teaching conditions in Shanghai shape how teachers engage in classroom instruction and thus shape what and how students learn as I have described above. Teachers are considered a national resource in China, and the government invests its resources, establishes its schooling systems, and recognizes accomplishments to support, develop, and reward this important work force. But it is also true that parents invest heavily in their children's education. Even in families where resources are limited, the success of their children through education is highly valued and the family lives out these values through investing their time and money on tutoring, shadow education programs, and long hours of homework. It is also true that Chinese students by and large hold a mindset that hard work matters and that their innate ability is not a limitation to the potential of their success in school—as many students in Western cultures are brought up to believe. Students with this mindset and with encouragement and demand from their families work hard in school and push themselves to do what their teachers ask them to do. And, finally, it is also true that Shanghai teachers work to ensure that all students meet the basic expectations of learning. They, too, hold a mindset that with enough hard work the students can master the basics. To many, the PISA results show exactly this, Shanghai students have shown that they have mastered the basics that their teachers expect of them.

As the nation calls for its students to develop a greater sense of innovation and creativity, it is also calling for teaching to support the individual interests of the students, to be supportive of problem-posing and problem-solving ways of learning, and to integrate knowledge across multiple disciplines. The culture of school learning in China has traditionally been driven by high-fstakes examinations as gate-keeping and placement metrics for Chinese students. The perception that the examination system creates a fair and merit-based opportunity for upward socioeconomic mobility supports the maintenance of this system among families. The cultural expectations of effort-based success that is objectively quantified in test results is currently living in tension with the policy and reform drive for schooling outcomes that rely on engagement and criterion-based performance assessment of students. Shanghai is currently exceeding at the traditional measures of student performance, partially due to the sophisticated and well-supported collective teaching practices within schools. Yet, Shanghai educators are not satisfied with what its students currently can do and how they can think. The policy path has been set down toward a more progressive pedagogy that is focused on student engagement in complex projects with uncertain outcomes. How these policy expectations will interact with the cultural expectations of school success and the well-honed teaching and learning practices in schools will be a challenge for the educational system to address.

REFERENCES

Aggarwal, D. (December 12, 2013). Innovating entrepreneurship: Teach for China. Huffington Post. Retrieved from http://www.huffingtonpost.com/china-hands/innovating-entrepreneursh_b_4488317.html

All-China Women's Federation (2013). Report on the state of rural children whose parents leave their hometown for making a living and rural-to-city migrant children in China. Retrieved from http://acwf.people.com.cn/n/2013/0510/c9901 3-21437965.html

The Asia Society (April 27, 2010). *China's 2020 Education Reform Strategy.* http://asiasociety.org/education/learning-world/chinas-2020-education-reform-strategy

The Asia Society (2010) *Shanghai: The World's Best School System.* http://asia-society.org/education/learning-world/shanghai-worlds-best-school-system

Burningham, G. (May 1, 2014). Lessons from the world's best public school. *Newsweek.* Retrieved from http://www.newsweek.com/2014/05/09/shanghai-high-confidential-249224.html

Center for International Education Benchmarking. http://www.ncee.org/programs-affiliates/center-on-international-education-benchmarking/top-performing-countries/shanghai-china/

Center for International Education Study. http://www.cnsaes.org/homepage/saes_jybgjjyyjyzxzx/eindex.htm

Chen, Y., & Feng, S. (2012). Migrant schools and the education of migrant children in China: Learning versus institutional barriers. Working paper. Shanghai University of Finance and Economics, School of Economics. Retrieved from http://www.lepp.zju.edu.cn/upload/2013-05/13053119046814.pdf

Chen, X. (2012, March 6). Government to raise education spending to 4% of GDP. China Daly. Retrieved from http://www.chinadaily.com.cn/china/2012-03/06/content_14762592.htm

Cheng, K. (2014, June 6). Does culture matter? Education reforms in East Asia. *Revue internationale d'éducation de Sèvres.* Retrieved from http://ries.revues.org/3804

Cheng, K. & Yip, H. (2006, October). Facing the knowledge Society: Reforming secondary education in Hong Kong and Shanghai. Education Working Paper Series No. 5. The World Bank.

China Education Center (n.d.). Primary and Secondary Education. Retrieved from http://www.chinaeducenter.com/en/cedu/psedu.php

China Education and Research Network (2001). Teacher Education in China. Retrieved from: http://www.edu.cn/HomePage/english/education/teachedu/introduction/index.shtml

China Household Finance Survey, Survey and Research Center for China Household Finance (2013). Southwestern University of Finance and Economics, Chengdu, China. Retrieved from http://www.chfsdata.org/detail-19-30.html

China Labor Bulletin (December 2014). Teachers' strikes escalates across China. Retrieved from http://www.clb.org.hk/en/content/teachers%E2%80%99-strikes-escalate-across-china

Chinese Teacher Development Foundation. http://www.jsjjh.org.cn/jsjjh/js/jjhjj.shtml

Communist Party of China Central Committee and State Council (2014). *National new urbanization plan* (2014–2020). Retrieved from http://www.gov.cn/gongbao/content/2014/content_2644805.htm

Communist Party of China Central Committee (1985). *The Decision on Education Reform.* http://www.moe.edu.cn/publicfiles/business/htmlfiles/moe/moe_177/200407/2482.html

Communist Party of China Central Committee and the State Council. (1993). *Chinese education reform and development outline.* Retrieved from http://www.moe.edu.cn/publicfiles/business/htmlfiles/moe/moe_177/200407/2484.html

Dalian Diary Blog (June 1, 2007). 12 Differences Between Chinese Education and American Education. Retrieved from http://slkchina.wordpress.com/2007/06/01/12-differences-between-chinese-education-and-american-education/

Database of laws and regulations (China). http://www.npc.gov.cn/englishnpc/Law/Frameset-index.html

Fu, J. (2010, March 2). Urban-rural income gap widest since reform. China Daily. Retrieved from http://www.chinadaily.com.cn/china/2010-03/02/content_9521611.htm

Gang, D. (Ed.) (2010). *National survey and policy analysis for teacher professional development in primary and secondary schools.* Shanghai: East China Normal University Press.

Gang, D., & Meilu, S. (2007). The qualifications of the teaching force in China (pp. 19–27). In R.Ingersoll (Ed.), *A Comparative Study of Teacher Preparation and Qualifications in Six Nations.* Philadelphia, PA: Consortium for Policy Research in Education.

Gao, H. (January 23, 2014). *Shanghai test scores and the mystery of the missing children.* Sinosphere: Dispatches from China. Retrieved from http://sinosphere.blogs.nytimes.com/2014/01/23/shanghai-test-scores-and-the-mystery-of-the-missing-children/

Gopinathan, S., Tan, S., Yanping, F., Devi, L., Ramos, C., & Chao, E. (2008). *Transforming teacher education: Redefined professional for 21st century schools*. Singapore: The International Alliance of Leading Institutes.

Information Office of the Shanghai Municipality (April 1, 2012). Shanghai's 12th Five-Year Plan for Educational Reform and Development: press conference highlights. Retrieved from http://en.shio.gov.cn/press-con/2012/04/01/1151817.html.

Ingersoll, R. (2007). *A Comparative Study of Teacher Preparation and Qualifications in Six Nations*. Philadelphia, PA: Consortium for Policy Research in Education.

Li, P., Li, Q., Sun, L. (2004). *Social stratification in China today*. Beijing: Social Sciences Documentation Publishing House.

International Alliance of Leading Education Institutes (2008). *Transforming Teacher Education: Redefined Professionals for 21st Century Schools*, Singapore: National Institute of Education. Retrieved from http://website.education.wisc.edu/inei/wp-content/uploads/Documents/Transforming_Teacher_Education_Report.pdf

Jensen, B. & Farmer, J. (2013, May). School turnaround in Shanghai: The empowered-management program approach to improving school performance. Center for American Progress.

Jiang, X. (August 1, 2011). How Shanghai schools beat the all. *The Diplomat*. Retrieved November 1, 2013 from http://thediplomat.com/2011/08/01/how-shanghai-schools-beat-them-all/

Liang, S., Glaz, S., DeFranco, T., Vinsonhaler, C., Grenier, R., & Cardetti, F. (2012). An examination of the preparation and practice of grades 7–12 mathematics teachers from the Shandong Province in China. *Journal of Mathematics Teacher Education*, 15(5).

Loveless, T. (2013, December 11). Attention OECD-PISA: Your silence on China is wrong. The Brown Center Chalkboard No. 48. The Brookings Institution. Retrieved from http://www.brookings.edu/research/papers/2013/12/11-shanghai-pisa-scores-wrong-loveless?rssid=brown&utm_source=feedburner&utm_medium=feed&utm_campaign=Feed%253A%2bBrookingsRSS%252Fcenters%252Fbrown%2b%28Brookings%2bCenters%2b-%2bBrown%2bCenter%2bon%2bEducation%2bPolicy%29

Ministry of Education. Education Laws. http://www.moe.gov.cn/jyb_xxgk/xxgk_jyfl/flfg_jyfl/

Ministry of Education (2105). *Education in China—2013 National Educa-tion Development*. Retrieved from http://www.moe.edu.cn/jyb_sjzl/s5990/201503/t20150331_186797.html

Ministry of Education (2015). State Council on the issuance of a village teacher support program (2015–2020). Retrieved from http://www.moe.edu.cn/publicfiles/business/htmlfiles/moe/s7058/201506/188990.html

Ministry of Education (2014). http://www.moe.edu.cn/

Ministry of Education (2003). *Education Statistics 2003*. http://www.moe.gov.cn/.

Ministry of Education (2005). *Basic Statistics of Regular Schools in China*. http://www.moe.gov.cn/.

Ministry of Education (1999). *The Action Plan to Revitalize Education in the Twenty-first Century*. Beijing, China: Beijing Normal University.

National Center for Economics and Education (n.d.). Shanghai-China. Center on International Education Benchmarking. Retrieved from: http://www.ncee.org/programs-affiliates/center-on-international-education-bench-marking/top-performing-countries/shanghai-china/

New York Times (January 16, 2013). "In education, China takes the lead." Business day report. Retrieved from: http://www.nytimes.com/interactive/2013/01/16/business/In-Education-China-Takes-the-Lead.html?ref=business&_r=0

Niu, Z., & Liu, M. (2012). *Teacher merit pay in China: A case study in Beijing*. Paper presented at the annual meeting of the 56th Annual Conference of the Comparative and International Education Society, Caribe Hilton, San Juan, Puerto Rico.

Organization for Economic Co-operation and Development (OECD) (n.d.). Programme for International Student Assessment (PISA): About PISA. Retrieved from http://www.oecd.org/pisa/aboutpisa/.

Organization for Economic Co-operation and Development (OECD) (2011). Education at a glance 2011 Country note-China. DOI: http://dx.doi.org/10.1787/eag-2011-en

Organization for Economic Co-operation and Development (OECD) (2015). *OECD Economic Surveys" China*. OECD Publishing, Paris. http://dx.doi.org/10.1787/eco_surveys-chn-2015-en

Organization for Economic Co-operation and Development (OECD) (2014a). *PISA 2012 Results in Focus: What 15-year-olds know and what they can do with what they know*. (Overview), PISA, OECD Publishing. Retrieved from http://www.oecd.org/pisa/keyfindings/pisa-2012-results-overview.pdf

Organization for Economic Co-operation and Development (OECD) (2014b). *PISA 2012 Results: What Students Know and Can Do – Student Perfor-mance in Mathematics, Reading and Science* (Volume I, Revised edition,

February 2014), PISA, OECD Publishing. DOI: http://dx.doi
.org/10.1787/9789264201118-en

Organization for Economic Co-operation and Development (OECD) (2014c).
*PISA 2012 Results: Excellence through Equity: Giving Every Student
the Chance to Succeed* (Volume II), PISA, OECD Publishing. DOI: http://
dx.doi.org/10.1787/9789264201132-en

Organization for Economic Co-operation and Development (OECD) (2010).
Shanghai and Hong Kong: Two Distinct Examples of Education Reform
in China" in the publication, *Strong Performers and Successful Reformers
in Education: Lessons from PISA for the United States.* Retrieved from
http://www.oecd.org/edu/school/programmeforinternationalstudentas-
sessmentpisa/strongperformersandsuccessfulreformersineducationlessons-
frompisafortheunitedstates.htm

Paine, L. W., Fang, Y., & Wilson, S. (2003). Entering a culture of teaching.
In T. Britton, L. W. Paine, D. Pimm, and S. Raizen (Eds.), *Comprehensive
teacher induction: Systems for early career learning* (pp. 20–82). Nether-
lands: Kluwer Academic.

Paine, L., & Ma, L. (1993). Teachers working together: A dialogue on organizational and cultural perspectives of Chinese teachers. *International
Journal of Educational Research*, 19(8), 675–697.

Phoenix Education (2015, July 30). The Ministry of Education released 2014
National Educational Development Statistical Bulletin. Retrieved from
http://edu.ifeng.com/a/20150730/41406904_0.shtml

Roberts, D. (April 4, 2013). Chinese education: The truth behind the boasts.
Bloomberg Businessweek (Global Economics). Retrieved from: http://
www.businessweek.com/articles/2013-04-04/chinese-education-the-truth-
behind-the-boasts#p2

Salleh, H., & Tan, C. (2013). Novice teachers learning from others: Mentoring in Shanghai schools. *Australian Journal of Teacher Education*, 38(3).
DOI: 10.14221/ajte.2013v38n3.1

Shanghai Municipal Information Office Press Conference (March 28, 2012).
Shanghai's 12th five-year plan for educational reform and development.
Retrieved from http://en.shio.gov.cn/presscon/2012/04/01/1151817.html

Shanghai Municipal Statistics Bureau (2011). *Shanghai Basic Facts.* Shanghai:
Information Office of Shanghai Municipality.

Shanghai Municipal Statistics Bureau (2014). *Shanghai Statistical Yearbook.*
Retrieved from http://www.stats-sh.gov.cn/data/toTjnj.xhtml?y=2014e

Shanghai Municipal Statistics Bureau (2015). Statistical communique of Shanghai economic and social development 2014. Retrieved from http://www.
stats-sh.gov.cn/sjfb/201502/277392.html

Shanghai Normal University, Department of Education. http://ec.shnu.edu.cn/
    Default.aspx?tabid=4299&language=zh-CN

Shanghai Statistical Yearbook (2014). China Statistics Press: Shanghai, China.

Simon, K. (March, 13, 2015). Private schools, on the rise in China, are now in
    Beijing's 'crosshairs'. Asia Society Worldwide. Retrieved from
    http://asiasociety.org/blog/asia/private-schools-rise-china-are-now-bei-
    jings-crosshairs

Tan, C. (2013). *Learning from Shanghai: Lessons on achieving educational
    success*. Springer: Dordrecht.

Teach for All. Retrieved from http://www.teachforall.org/en

Teach for China. http://www.tfchina.org/en/index.aspx

Tucker, M. (2014). *Chinese lessons: Shanghai's rise to the top of the PISA
    league tables*. Washington, DC: National Center on Education and the
    Economy.

UNESCO (2011). World data on education: People's Republic of China, 7th
    Ed. Retrieved from http://www.ibe.unesco.org/fileadmin/user_upload/Pub-
    lications/WDE/2010/pdf-versions/China.pdf

UNESCO (2014). Country Profiles: China. Retrieved from: http://www.uis.
    unesco.org/DataCentre/Pages/country-profile.aspx?code=CHN&regionc
    ode=40515

United Nations Children's Fund: National Working Committee on Children
    and Women & National Bureau of Statistics (2014). *Children in China:
    an atlas of social indicators*. Beijing: UNICEF Office for China.

Wang, L., & Holland, T. (2011). In search of educational equity for the
    migrant children of Shanghai, *Comparative Education*, 47(4), 471–487.

Wang, Z. (January 5, 2009). Wen Jiabao pledges school reform to counter
    economic crisis, Asia News. http://www.asianews.it/index.php?l=en&art=
    14138&geo=6&size=A#

We like to move it move it. (2012, February 25). *The Economist*. Retrieved
    from http://www.economist.com/node/21548277

The World Bank. Retrieved from http://data.worldbank.org/indicator/SP.POP
    .TOTL

The World Bank (2015). Data. Retrieved from: http://data.worldbank.org/indi-
    cator/SE.PRM.GINT.FE.ZS/countries

The World Bank. (2014, June). China economic update. Retrieved from http://
    www.worldbank.org/content/dam/Worldbank/document/EAP/China/
    China_Economic_Update_June2014.pdf

The World Bank. Poverty and Equity. Retrieved from http://povertydata.world-
    bank.org/poverty/country/CHN

The World Population Review. Retrieved from http://worldpopulationreview
    .com/world-cities/shanghai-population/

Ye, Lan (2009). "New Basic Education" and me: Retrospective notes from the past ten years of research. *Frontiers of Education in China*, 4(4) 558–609. DOI 10.1007/s11516–009–0031–0

Zhang, J. (2014, July 30). China focus: Hukou reforms to help 100mil-lino Chinese. CCTV.com Retrieved http://english.cntv.cn/2014/07/30/ARTI1406711906970602.shtml

Zhang, M. (December 19, 2013). Shanghai responds to school ranking cheating allegations. The Asia Society. Retrieved from http://asiasociety.org/blog/asia/shanghai-responds-school-ranking-cheating-allegations

Zhang, M., Xu, J., Sun, C. (2014). Effective teachers for successful schools and high performing students: The case of Shanghai. In S. K. Lee, W. O. Lee, & E. L. Low (Eds.), *Educational Policy Innovations: Levelling Up and Sustaining Educational Achievement* (pp. 143–161). Springer Education Innovation Book Series 1: Singapore. DOI 10.1007/978–981–4560–08–5_9

Zhao, X. (May, 5, 2014). School tests blamed for suicides. China Daily. Retrieved from http://www.chinadaily.com.cn/china/2014-05/14/content_17505291.htm

Zhicheng, W. (2009). Wen Jiabao pledges school reform to counter economic crisis. AsiaNews.it. Retrieved from http://www.asianews.it/index.php?l=en&art=14138&geo=6&size=A

Zhu, X. & Han, X. (2006). Reconstruction of the teacher education system in China. *International Education Journal*, 7(1). 66–73.

Printed in the United States
By Bookmasters